A Soft Whisper

Olive Peynado

TRILOGY CHRISTIAN PUBLISHERS
TUSTIN, CA

Trilogy Christian Publishers
A Wholly Owned Subsidiary of Trinity Broadcasting Network
2442 Michelle Drive
Tustin, CA 92780

A Soft Whisper

Trilogy Christian Publishers A Wholly Owned Subsidiary of Trinity Broadcasting Network
2442 Michelle Drive Tustin, CA 92780

Cover design by Jeff Summers

For information about special discounts for bulk purchases, please contact Trilogy Christian Publishing.

Manufactured in the United States of America

10 9 8 7 6 5 4 3 2 1

Library of Congress Cataloging-in-Publication Data is available.

ISBN: 978-1-68556-230-4

E-ISBN: 978-1-68556-231-1

Dedication

To my husband, Franklin, my best friend, whose love, prayers, patience, and support encouraged me during the writing of this book. To my daughters, Bevoni and Wendy, who believed in me, prayed for me, and encouraged me throughout the writing process. You never doubted I could do this, thank you.

To my grandchildren Kaelan, Katrianna, Kymorah, Ksena and Amariah, Jediah, and Josiah, who inspired me to write stories that would show God's love and faithfulness. Your thirst for books that encouraged and demonstrated Christlike principles in children and teens was why this book was written. May you glorify our Lord and Savior Jesus Christ in your schools and college as you demonstrate His love to others through your words and actions.

Katrianna, may you use your writing gift to one day write stories that will inspire others.

And to all the children, teens, or adults who will read this book, I trust it will minister to those who are seeking to live a Christ-centered life and give hope to others who have broken hearts and wounded spirits. I trust this story will encourage a thirst for God that will transform your lives.

This book is dedicated to my grandchildren; I thank God for all of you.

Acknowledgements

Special thanks to my friend Althea Meyers Williams for the countless hours spent editing the book in its raw stage.

To my grandchildren Katrianna and Kymorah Morrissey, who read and critiqued the draft of this book. Thank you for your insights and suggestions given from a teenager's perspective.

To my siblings Rosemarie, Angella, Jennifer, Bosworth, Melville, my sister-in-law Caryll Dawn, and to my dear friends Irving, Joyce, Paula, Beverly, Phyllis, Blossom, and Jacqueline, who encouraged and prayed for me through the completion of this project.

Most importantly, I give glory and honor to the Lord Jesus Christ, who is my guide and helper and without whom I would not be able to write this book. To Him be glory and honor.

Contents

Chapter 1

Maria came through the front door, dropped her book bag on the kitchen table, and sighed. She was utterly frustrated. She had tried so hard not to get into trouble at school, but there she was again in another verbal confrontation. What would she tell her mother? That she had difficulty controlling her temper? That surely would not work. She mused over the teachings of her mother and recalled the many times she had told her to walk away; however, that was impossible, or so Maria thought. How could she speak kindly to someone who was always picking on her and saying nasty things about her and her family? She just could not bring herself to do that. *Mom must have "knocked" her head,* she thought. "A soft answer turneth away wrath, but grievous words stir up anger" (Proverbs 15:1, KJV). What does that really mean?

Her thoughts were interrupted by the opening of the front door. Jamie, Maria's older brother, came in, ruffled her hair playfully, and asked, "How was your day? You look as if you have the weight of the world on your shoulder. Lighten up, girl, and live."

She looked up at Jamie and said, "I was in a fight again today; I am sure to be in trouble with Mom. She does not understand the pressure I am under. I am always being bullied at school. I have told the teacher, and nothing has been done about it. Well, that is how I feel. I get so angry that I lash out and, before I know it, I am in a verbal battle, and I feel I have to find some way to insult them."

Jamie sat down at the kitchen table and invited Maria to join him. He wanted to hear all that happened at school today to have caused his little sister to be so upset and to react in such a manner. Maria started to sob, "I miss Daddy so much. Things were perfect when he was here. Now I feel as if we are missing a link in the family chain; part of it is gone, and I cannot fill that void."

Jamie and Maria's father was a successful businessman who owned several flower shops. It seemed as if everyone in Palm Beach County knew Carlos Rodriquez and his beautiful wife, Karla. Karla was strikingly beautiful with brown eyes, long dark brown hair, long shapely legs, and a beautiful tan complexion. Jamie got his striking looks and beautiful complexion from his mother. Maria looked more like her father, who was short, had brown complexion, a flat nose, and unruly curly black hair. His customers at the flower shop would joke with him and ask him how he had managed to capture such a beauty. "Look at yourself, Carlos," they would joke, "how could Karla fall for you?" Carlos' response was always the same, "She fell for my good looks and personality." They would all laugh together because Carlos was not a handsome man, but his personality made up for his looks. His creative and artistic ability was seen in his bouquets, and he was widely sought out to decorate venues for special occasions. Mr. Rodriquez was known for his warm smile and endearing, encouraging words and was regarded by many as a generous, wise, and humble man who embraced and loved people regardless of their status in life.

Carlos worked hard to make his family comfortable but did not save much; he spent a lot of money on the home, his wife, and the kids. It was his joy to provide for his family and make them happy. Their father had been having chest pains for a few months but did not take them seriously; he just passed it off as indigestion. Dad was good at caring for everyone else but did not take care of himself. He went to work as usual one morning and never came home. The chest pains started and steadily became worse; by the time he got to St. Mary's hospital, it was too late. Their dad had died from a heart attack, thus leaving Mom with both children to raise on her own. Mom tried to keep the flower shop open, but she had no experience running a business, she had no creative bone in her body, and the business failed, so Mom had to go back to work. This meant that she was no longer at home when the children got home from school, there was no hot meal waiting for them, and dinner conversations were now fewer and further in between.

Maria reminded Jamie of how energetic, humorous, and full of life their father was. She loved when he was home; he called her his little angel. This made her feel special. Life then was so good.

She burst into tears again and shouted, "Why did Daddy have to die?"

"One never knows why these things happen, Pumpkin, but we can't just curl up and die. I miss Daddy too, and sometimes, I cry myself to sleep wishing he was here. We must move on; he will always be cherished, and he will remain in our memories forever."

There was silence for a while, then Jamie said, "We have to support Mom now more than ever. She has been working so hard and not getting enough rest; we do not want to lose her too. Let us see how best we can help her." Maria agreed and suggested that they start by keeping their rooms and the house clean, and instead of Mom coming home to prepare dinner for the family, they would prepare dinner so that when Mom comes home, she would have a hot meal. This would allow them to spend more time with her, and she would not be so tired. They also thought that on the weekends, they would do the laundry; that would give their mom time to rest in between jobs. They were so excited and decided that they would not tell her of their plan; they would just do what they had committed to do and surprise her.

"Sounds like a good plan to me," Jamie said. "Let us do it." Jamie felt their mom had a really difficult time managing the home and work, and Maria thought that she was not making it any easier on her mother when she got into fights, and the teacher called home. *This certainly added to her stress*, Maria thought. Jamie broke in on her thoughts, "I've got to go do my homework, and I have to study for a test tomorrow. See you later."

Maria went back to thinking about the whole situation and decided if she was going to help to relieve some of the stress she had caused her mother. She would begin by changing the way she reacted and responded to others. She decided that from now on, she would try to set an example at school, and when other students make fun of her, she would respond with kindness.

I wonder if that is what is meant by "A soft answer turneth away wrath, but grievous words stir up anger," Maria asked herself. *I must remember to ask Mom about this, but let us not think this is going to be easy. This is going to be a very difficult challenge, she mused.*

That clique of girls, Terry, Angie, Brianna, and Lori, think they are better than everyone else. They pick on me because I choose not to dress like them, and I do not use profanity. "Goody

Two-Shoes" they call me. Daddy always told me to look for the best in other people and not to focus on the bad, that I should find ways in which to complement others. These girls surely make this hard, she thought. But I am going to try my best. I am going to make Mom proud of me. I had better go do my homework, so I am all done when Mom gets home.

Maria completed her homework and decided to wait up for her mother. She longed to spend some time with her, just to talk and laugh the way they used to. Also, it would be nice to concentrate on someone else for a change and ask Mom about her day. Maybe Mom also had challenges on her job, and it would be good to think about her instead of always centering on herself. Her thoughts went back to some of the times she had spent conversing with Dad. He certainly was a wise man. He had told her many times that she should remember that life was not all about her, that she should always put others first. That did not stop him from pampering her, but Dad always practiced what he preached; he was always looking out for others. She never could understand that, but now it dawned on her that Mom also had difficulties and maybe needed some encouragement too. She needed to be less self-centered and put her mother first.

Her thoughts were interrupted by the key turning in the door. She ran to the door to greet her mom and to help her with the bags. She hugged her and said, "Mom, have I told you lately how much I love you? I feel blessed to have you as my mom. I do appreciate all you are doing to make ends meet. Let me take your shoes."

"Oh, baby, that's nice," she reacted with a faint smile.

"I am sure your feet are tired, and you need to put them up for a while. I long to sit and talk with you like old times."

"Really?"

She nodded and said, "Yeah. Maybe, when you're off on Sunday, we can have some of those special times we used to have as a family, laughing, talking, and just goofing off. But first, you must be hungry and tired after a long day at work. Let me heat the dinner up for you."

Maria got the dinner on the table and sat down with her mom; she watched her as she slowly ate her dinner. She looked so tired that eating looked like a chore. At this point, Maria decided she would tell her mother one of her and Jamie's plans.

"Mom, tomorrow morning you don't have to get up and cook breakfast for us before you leave for work. Jamie and I will also prepare dinner when we get home from school, so when you get home, you will have a hot meal waiting on you. Take the time to get some more rest in the morning before you go to work. Just tell us what you want us to prepare, and we will have it done for you."

Mom got up and hugged Maria; with tears in her eyes, she thanked her for being so thoughtful. "It would be nice to sleep in sometimes. I cannot remember the last time I was able to have a good night's rest. You are such good kids. I am thankful for both of you; you bring joy to my life. Without you, I don't know how I would be able to bear the death of your father, but when I see you and Jamie, I see a little bit of him in both of you, and now I see you practicing some of the things he taught you. You are showing selflessness. Thank you."

Maria felt so happy she hugged Mom again and suggested that Mom go to bed and not worry about them because everything would be alright. She bade her mother good night and went to her room.

Maria got into bed, happy she had spent that little time with Mom. She prayed she would have a good day at school tomorrow and made up her mind that if she was provoked, she would put into practice the things her dad had taught her. She would think before she speaks; she would "weigh" her words carefully. Would her words damage, or would they heal? It sure felt good to think about someone else for a change. She slid down in her bed, pulled her comforter up to her chin, grateful she had a loving family and a warm bed in which to sleep. She listened to the rain "making music" on the roof and thought this was the perfect time to be in bed. Life was not so bad after all.

Chapter 2

The alarm went off, and Maria groaned as she turned in bed and pulled the covers over her head. She wished she had another hour to sleep; it felt as if she had just closed her eyes. She had laid awake for quite some time thinking about all that had transpired that day and how she could put in practice what she had determined she would do. She jumped out of bed as she heard Mom call, reminding her it was time to get up.

This was going to be a wet day; she could hear the rain falling on the roof. She loved the rain when she was in bed, but heading out in it was not something she looked forward to. Although she enjoyed watching the rain come down, getting wet was another matter. What she loved most was what came after the rain, the lovely rainbow. Dad would always say that the rainbow was a symbol of God's love for us and a sign of a promise He made to us after a flood. What was that flood again? Is there really a God? Well, Dad believed it, and so does Mom, and it is in the Bible, so it must be true.

Maria snapped out of her daydreaming, rushed to the bathroom, took a shower, and got dressed for school. She ran downstairs and found that Jamie had prepared breakfast, eaten, and was heading out the door as he grabbed a jacket. Jamie attended Patterson High School, which was close to home, so he walked to school, but Maria had to take the bus. Ferris Middle School was three miles from home and started later than his school.

"Hurry up, Pumpkin; it is almost time to leave. You need to get up earlier, so you can sit and have a proper breakfast. This is the most important meal of the day," Mom said. Maria pulled on her coat, grabbed a banana, an apple, and her bags, and shouted to Mom that she was sorry she could not stop to have the breakfast Jamie had prepared. However, she would just eat the banana and apple on her way to the bus stop. After all, her teacher had told her that banana was "brain food," so she should be okay with that, she thought. As she ran to catch the bus, Maria's mind ran on the girls who were always tormenting her. *Will they pick on me today? If so, I must remember to choose my words carefully because "a soft answer turns away wrath, but grievous words stir up anger." I can never understand why people choose to put others down, but I must remember to respond with kindness,* she thought. Would this be easier said than done?

Maria got to the bus stop as it pulled up. The run through the rain was not too bad—she had made it just in time. "Hey, come sit beside me," John called as she boarded the bus. She was happy to see him, as he did not ride the bus every day. His mom sometimes drove him to school when she was working in that area. John was her friend from elementary school, and they had similar upbringing and values. Their parents were friends, his dad used to be her dad's best friend, and his mom had known her mom since high school. They also attended the same church, although they had not attended for quite a while. It was a relief to see him; he was her protector on the bus.

John was handsome with large brown eyes and hair that fell on his face, sometimes hiding his eyes. He had a habit of passing his hand through his hair as he brushed it away from his eyes. Maria would tease him about it, and she wondered why he did not cut it, but then again, it made him look kind of cute. John was also bigger and stronger than most of the guys his age and would always stand up for her. He was a real gentleman. The boys at school did not even know what a gentleman was, much less know the attributes of one. Terry, one of her "tormentors," was on the bus, but this did not matter because she would not dare say anything to her with John sitting beside her. John was known to defend others who were being taken advantage of, and everyone knew John was her friend.

The ride to school would be good after all. They chatted all the way, and Maria shared some of the daily challenges she faced from her "tormentors," as she called them, Terry, Angie, Brianna, and Lori. She also told him that she had resolved to treat them with respect, respond with kindness, and shared what her dad had taught her: to never respond with harshness but always respond kindly to others.

All too soon, the bus ride to school came to an end. They got off the bus, and John encouraged her to be strong, gave her a quick hug, and ran off to his class. *Now it is showtime,* Maria thought; she anticipated what the day would be like as she walked slowly to math class. She loved math and did very well at it. At times she thought some of the other students were jealous of her because math was so easy for her. This she owed to Mr. Jones, her math teacher, who made math interesting.

Mr. Jones was a tall, skinny man who looked a bit eccentric. She wondered if he had a wife because his clothes were never color coordinated. It appeared that he had eyes in the back of his head because he would call on a student who was talking without looking around, and he easily identified students who were not listening. Some of the students thought he was strange, but she loved him as a teacher. He enjoyed teaching and used many props to teach each new concept, which made math easy to understand. His enthusiasm for the subject caused her to fall in love with math.

Maria grasped new concepts easily, and Mr. Jones frequently asked her and a few other students to assist those who were having difficulty when she had completed her assignments. After he taught a new topic, Mr. Jones would work through problems on the board. Then, he placed the students in small groups, which he called tutorial groups. In each group, there was at least one student who understood the concept taught; that student would work with the group to guide them and answer any additional questions they might have. He moved around the groups, giving additional instruction if needed and giving additional problems to groups who were finished ahead of time. He would then work individually with students who had a hard time grasping a specific concept. Maria looked forward to those times because she loved explaining and helping others overcome their mathematical challenges.

Her thoughts were interrupted by Terry and Angie shouting, "Goody Two-Shoes, how are you doing?"

Maria responded, "Very well, thank you."

"Very well, thank you," they mimicked. "And who does she think she is? Very well, thank you. Always thinking that she is better than others."

Why did I answer like that? Maria thought. It might have been better just to say okay. Maria entered the classroom feeling a bit upset. The two girls were also in the same math class and, if they kept this up, it would prove to be a challenge responding kindly every time they "tried" her. Maria wondered what had happened to Lori; she had not been in class for three days. *Well, I guess it is better to have two tormentors in class than three. I am not going to allow those girls to get the better of me, so I will try to respond with kindness every time they say something rude to me,* she thought.

Angie was a tall, skinny Caucasian girl with brown hair who dressed in the latest fashion and wore brand-name clothes and shoes. She spent her time in class looking in the mirror and making sure her hair was in order. It seemed that she cared about her appearance far more than her education. Her grades showed it, and some of the students called her "airhead." With all the makeup that she wore, Maria thought she could do with a bit more color on her cheeks. Terry, on the other hand, was a beautiful, chocolate-colored girl with a smooth skin tone. She needed no make-up to make herself pretty, and she appeared to be smart but chose to play dumb. Maria wondered why she felt the need to be part of this group. Lori was blond and petite with beautiful blue eyes. Sometimes, Maria thought she saw a hint of sadness in her eyes and wondered what brought on that sadness. It seemed she was trying hard to disguise her true self, and Maria wondered why.

The bell rang, and Maria settled down to complete the math problem that was on the board. Mr. Jones believed in getting to work immediately after one was seated, and he expected to see each student trying to solve the problem on the whiteboard. At the beginning of the school year, Mr. Jones had shared with the class his method of instruction and the reasoning behind the way he taught. The question he placed on the whiteboard prior to instruction was one review method he used. This provided him with enough information to steer the class or guide his instruction. From this, he could determine the students who understood the concept, how many students had problems with it, and each student's areas of weakness. Also, it informed him if he needed to review as a class, if the class needed additional problems for practice, if he would have to reteach the concept, or if he could move on to another concept. Maria liked Mr. Jones and admired his style of teaching. He was a good math teacher, and sometimes she thought if she ever became a teacher, she would like to be just like him.

"Maria," Mr. Jones called. "Would you please go to the board and solve the problem? Make sure you walk the class through the steps you are taking as you solve."

Maria jumped up. She knew Mr. Jones realized that she was daydreaming and had not begun the problem. He had a way of calling on students who were not paying attention to keep all his students engaged in the learning process. She went forward slowly, giving herself time to read the problem before she got to the board. She picked up the dry erase marker and began to work the problem. Fortunately for her, she understood how to work that equation, and she completed the problem explaining as she went along. She felt that was a close call and determined within herself that she would always pay attention so as not to be caught off guard again.

Her "tormentors," Terry and Angie, were not happy that she solved the problem correctly. They kept contorting their faces and rolling their eyes at her; she wondered if they would seek her out after class to harass her again. It was time for group work, and she found herself in a group with Terry. She wondered how this would play out, especially since she was given the responsibility of group leader. She knew she could help the other students in the group because she understood how to work the problems and was pretty good at explaining and demonstrating. She was amazed that Terry by herself was not so bad; she asked questions and worked to solve the problem. Time seemed to have flown by quickly because it seemed as if they had just started when she heard, "It is time to wrap up; go back to your seats and respond to the question on the board. You will hand your work to me on your way out."

Soon after the bell rang, Maria grabbed her bag, handed in the worked problem, and headed out the door. The rest of the day went by uneventfully; the announcement came on, the bell rang for dismissal, and she hurried to the bus loop and got on her bus. She looked forward to helping Jamie prepare dinner. As the bus pulled up to her stop, she bounced out and practically ran home, anxious to complete homework so she could help Jamie with dinner. She planned to wait up for Mom and spend at least ten minutes with her before going to bed.

When she got home, Jamie was completing his homework. Maria called out to him and asked him how his day was.

"Great, but I want to hear how your day was," he replied.

"Pretty good; I had no significant problems. Terry was placed in my math group, and I was surprised that there were no problems. We worked well together, and she even asked me questions. She is different when she is by herself. Maybe she is not a bad person after all; I wonder why she hangs out with that group of girls."

"Well, Pumpkin, one never knows why people make the choices they do. Sometimes, it is just wanting to belong, or having low self-esteem, or just feeling unloved. One never knows what a person is going through and why they choose to put others down. Maybe it makes them feel better about themselves."

"But I don't understand," Maria replied. "If they have these problems, I would think they would want to be nice to others, so others may be nice to them also."

"Don't worry your pretty head about that; just get your homework done. I'll soon be finished with my homework, and then I will season the chicken. When you are done, come and help me in the kitchen."

"Okay."

Maria quickly completed her homework and ran into the kitchen; the aroma of fried chicken had made its way up the stairs to her room, and it made her feel very hungry. "How can I help?" she asked.

"Well, you can make the salad and set the table; I already have the potatoes boiling. I am going to make mashed potatoes and a sweet sauce to go along with it. I am not sure if the sauce will come out alright, but I'm going to try to make it the way I see Mom makes it."

With both working as a team, the dinner was completed quickly. This was Mom's early night, so she was expected to walk through the door any minute now. They made sure everything was in order, and Jamie turned the kettle on so Mom could have a cup of Sleepytime tea when she arrived. She said it made her relax and helped her to sleep.

Soon they could hear the key turn in the door; Mom was home. They were both happy and excited at the same time, anticipating her reaction to the beautifully laid dining settings. It reminded them of the way things were before Dad passed.

Chapter 3

Mom pushed her way slowly through the door; they could see from her gait that she was not feeling well. "What's wrong, Mom?" Jamie rushed to her side.

"I am having a bad headache, and I am feeling rather dizzy. Can you make me a cup of tea?"

Jamie helped his mom into a chair; she laid her head on the back of the chair and closed her eyes. Maria rushed to dim the lights; she had heard that lights might cause headaches to worsen. This was not going according to plan at all. She became extremely worried about her mom, and she started thinking, *What if*. She dared not finish that thought. *Mom had to get better*. She had no recollection of any time that her mother had ever been ill before. This was scary. She could see that Jamie was concerned too. He made the cup of tea and brought it to her.

"Mom, let me help you to sit up." He helped her up and gave her the cup of tea.

"Don't you worry about me; I will be okay soon. I'm just a little bit tired. I have been overdoing things a bit, and I think I'm just suffering from fatigue."

"Well, Mom, you need to take a few days off and get some rest. You are the only one we have now, and we can't afford to lose you too," said Jamie.

"You won't be losing me soon; I have no plans of going anywhere," she responded, smiling as she looked him in the face. She then looked around and saw how beautiful the table was set and complimented them on the setting. The aroma of the food had greeted her as soon as she opened the door and knew the children had prepared a meal so she could have some rest. *What thoughtful children I have, she thought. I am so grateful for them, and I am so blessed to have them in my life.* She thanked them for preparing the meal and apologized for not being able to eat it. She suggested that they eat their dinner and put up her portion for tomorrow. She could have it for lunch. She planned to take a sick day. All she wanted now was the cup of tea and some crackers.

Jamie and Maria sat down to eat. This was not the happy occasion they had planned, but they thanked God that at least Mom was here and she would get some rest tomorrow. They watched as she drank her tea and ate the crackers Jamie had given her. He then suggested that she take some pain pills, which he gave to her. After taking them, Maria helped her to the bathroom and then to bed. In a matter of minutes, Mom had fallen asleep. Maria pulled the comforter up over her, turned the lights off, and closed the bedroom door behind her. She joined Jamie in the family room; he seemed to be very worried.

"Mom is always taking care of us; it is now time for us to take care of her," Maria said. "I will stay home with her tomorrow; she should not be alone." They both agreed. They decided that if Mom needed to take another day off, then Jamie would stay home that day. They decided to be up early to check on her and ensure that she had breakfast before Jamie went to school. They cleared the table and did the dishes, after which they both went to bed.

Jamie and Maria found it difficult to fall asleep, their minds were on their mother, and they wondered if she would be okay. Was it only fatigue, or was there something seriously wrong with her? They prayed that they would not lose her too. After tossing and turning for what seemed hours, they fell asleep.

The alarm went off, and Maria got out of bed and went to check on her mom, who was fast asleep, or so she thought. She tiptoed out of the room and went into the kitchen to get something to eat and wait for Jamie to come down for breakfast. Her thoughts were on Mom and how she could help to make her life easier. Jamie came bounding down the stairs.

"Hi, Pumpkin. Have you checked on Mom yet?"

"Oh, yes, she was fast asleep. Let us go check to see if she is awake so we can take her a cup of coffee."

They went quietly into the room, and Jamie leaned over to kiss his mom goodbye. As he leaned forward, he noticed that her face was pale, and she did not appear to be breathing. He shook her shoulders, crying out, "Mom, Mom, wake up." Maria whispered that he should not wake her, thinking she was still asleep.

Jamie burst into tears after checking her pulse. "Mom is not breathing," he screamed. "Call an ambulance!" Maria grabbed her phone; her hands were shaking as she dialed 911. The operator came on, and Maria began screaming on the phone, "My mother is not breathing!" The operator began to question her, but Maria kept shouting that she needed help.

"Do you hear me? My mother is not breathing."

"Calm down and give me your address so I can dispatch the paramedics, then you will have to try and administer CPR to your mother. Do you know anything about CPR?"

"No, but my brother Jamie knows a little about it," Maria responded.

"Put the phone on speaker, so I can instruct him and guide him through the process. I will stay on the line with you until the paramedics arrive." Under the guidance of the 911 operator, Jamie administered

CPR until the paramedics arrived. One ran in with a machine, hooked it up to Mom while the other took over administering CPR. Another one came in with the gurney. It seemed as if they were working on her mom for hours, and nothing was happening.

Only five minutes had passed. Maria and Jamie began crying and screaming, "Mom, wake up, wake up, Mom, you can't leave us like Dad did. You're all we have; you can't do this to us." That is when they heard their mom cough; she had started to breathe. She had her eyes closed and was not talking, but she was breathing. The paramedic with the blond hair kept talking to their mom while they shifted her from the bed to the gurney. He told them that they would have to take their mother to the St. Mary's hospital in West Palm Beach and asked them if they had a relative they could call. They told them they did not have any relative who lived close by, but Mary was their mom's good friend, and they could call her, as they felt sure she would come. Mary was Karla's friend and John's mother. Jamie quickly made the call, and Mary said she would be right over to pick them up and take them to the hospital.

The paramedics took their mom to the hospital, and Jamie and Maria paced the floor while they waited for Mary to arrive. "Jamie, do you realize that Mom is going to the same hospital where they took Dad after his heart attack?"

"Yes, but Mom is not going to die. This is different."

"I hope so," Maria replied.

Both went back to pacing the floor. It seemed that it was taking Mary a long time to get to them. Impatient and worried, they just wanted to be with their mom, or at least at the hospital close to her. They wanted to know what was happening. The question "What if? What if? What if...?" was like a broken record playing over and over in their heads. No one was talking, each deep in their own thoughts. The doorbell rang, and they both ran to the door, pulling on their jackets and grabbing the keys. Locking the door, they ran out to the car, jumped in, and broke down crying. Mary wanted to know what had happened. Jamie filled her in and told her they did not know the status of their mother, only that she was breathing, not talking, eyes closed, and that she had been taken to St. Mary's hospital. Maria asked what Dad would have done in a situation like this, and Mary responded, "Pray." She offered to pray with them. As she prayed, they prayed silently, asking God to heal their mom and not let her die. They kept repeating to themselves, "Please, God, do not let my mother die. Please, God, do not let my mother die."

The car pulled up to the entrance of the emergency room; the kids jumped out and ran into the emergency room and rushed up to the desk, enquiring about their mom. By then, Mary had parked the car and had joined them. They were told that the doctors were with her and that either the doctor or a nurse would soon be out to update them on their mother's condition. They sat down, held hands, and waited for a while, but Jamie got up; he just could not sit still: he felt helpless, his mom was ill, and there was nothing he could do for her. He paced the floor; it seemed as if he was making a pattern in the floor, taking the same steps, the same route repeatedly.

One hour went by before a doctor came to speak to them. He introduced himself as Dr. Charles and informed them that their mom had a minor heart attack and that preliminary test had revealed their mom had a blockage in one of her arteries. He told them that he would be taking their mom into surgery to clear the blockage and explained that he would be performing an angioplasty, which would include putting stents in the affected artery, which would keep the artery open so blood would flow normally from the heart to the rest of the body. He informed them that he would return after the procedure to update them and that they would be able to see their mother at that time. Jamie thanked the doctor, and they settled down to wait for the procedure to end.

It seemed an eternity before Dr. Charles returned to inform them that she had two blockages, not just one. The blockages were now cleared, and everything went well. They would keep her overnight for observation, and she would be discharged the following day. "Well, I guess you would like to see her now," the doctor said. "Follow me; I'll take you to her room." Jamie, Maria, and Mary thanked the doctor and followed him to their mom's room.

"Mom, you gave us a scare," Jamie said. "I would not like to go through that again." They hugged her, taking care not to squeeze her too much. She was happy to see them and apologized to them for giving them such a scare. They all agreed that she would have to take it easy now, although the doctor told her she could resume her normal activities in one week's time. Mom encouraged the children and her friend to go home and get some rest, and she would see them the next day. She was tired and wanted to rest. In addition, she wanted to have some time to reflect on the year that passed since her husband's death. In retrospect, she realized she had not taken time to grieve. She needed to get it out of her system. Karla always thought that she had to be strong for her children and never took the time to grieve; she had bottled up her feelings for so long, and now it was time to let it out. Alone in the hospital room, she allowed herself the luxury of grieving for her husband. For the first time since she had heard of his death, she felt that she could cry and cry and cry. This is exactly what she did.

Chapter 4

Mary and the children walked slowly to the car, each of them engrossed in their own thoughts but feeling grateful that their mom was alive. The silence was broken by Jamie saying, "We knew Mom was tired and something was wrong, we knew she needed rest, but this was not the type of rest we envisioned. We just have to thank God for saving her life." He burst out singing his mother's favorite song, "He's been faithful, faithful to me." Maria and Mary joined him, and, soon, all three of them were singing praises to God for His goodness. They felt a new sense of appreciation and gratitude to God for sparing their mother's life. The children knew they needed to spend more time in prayer and the Bible, and they needed to reflect God's beauty in their daily lives. Life was too short, and the unexpected could happen at any time; their lives could suddenly change again, just as they did when their dad died.

They drove home, each submerged in their own thoughts. The silence was broken by Mary informing them that they were home. She wanted to know if they would prefer to pack a bag and stay at her house, but they both declined. They wanted to be home. Jamie and Maria thanked Mary, exited the car, and entered their home. This would be a long night, and they were both tired, so they showered and went to bed.

Maria was startled out of her sleep as the alarm on her phone went off, signaling the need to get up and get dressed for school. She was surprised that she had slept for three hours and turned in her bed, wishing she had more time to sleep. Her thoughts went to her mom in the hospital, so she jumped out of bed and ran to the phone to call the hospital to check up on her mother. The call was placed to her mother's hospital room, who assured her that she was feeling much better and would be home that evening. Maria was excited; she purposed in her heart that she would not allow anything to steal the joy she felt that her mom was well enough to be discharged from the hospital. She would not allow her "tormentors" to cause her to "lose her cool," nothing could interfere with the feeling of gratitude she felt for her mother's recovery. "Jamie, Mom is coming home today. Mary will pick her up from the hospital and take her home. She will be home by the time you get home from school."

The smell of breakfast cooking floated up the stairs; Maria could feel her stomach growling, the aroma of eggs and bacon had alerted her stomach that she was hungry. Her brother shouted to her that breakfast was ready, and he was leaving for school. She hastily showered, dressed, and ran down the stairs, quickly ate her breakfast, grabbed her book bag, and ran to catch the bus. She could see the bus coming in the distance and wondered if she would make it to the bus stop in time. She arrived at the bus stop as the bus was pulling in at the stop; the students piled onto it. She boarded the bus, sat down panting from the run, and reminded herself that she would not allow anything or anyone to steal her joy. She looked around to see if her friend John was on the bus, but he was not. She wanted to update him on her mother's progress, and she needed someone to talk to.

Her mind went back to the trauma she went through with the sudden death of her father and was happy that the same thing did not happen to her mother. She was engrossed in her thoughts as the bus pulled up at another stop and did not notice Terry boarding the bus. Her thoughts were interrupted when Terry bounced her as she passed. "Goody Two-Shoes," she whispered. Maria reflected on the promise she made to herself not to get angry. She could hear her father's advice playing in her head, "A soft answer turneth away wrath, but grievous words stir up anger." She still did not fully understand what her dad had meant by those words; she knew it had to do with her getting angry because whenever she felt anger rising in her, those words would spring to her mind. *There must be an important lesson to learn from this, she thought. I wish I had asked Dad what he meant by those words, but it is now too late; he is not around for me to ask.* How she missed him.

The bus rolled into the bus loop, and the students began to pile out. Maria was deep in thought, not realizing that all the other students had left, and she was still sitting on the bus. Her thoughts were interrupted by Mr. James, the bus driver, telling her that she was at school and it was time to get off the bus and go to class. She jumped up, thanked him, and rushed off the bus not wanting to be late for her math class. This was her favorite class, and Mr. Jones was her favorite teacher. He made math "come to life," and she enjoyed his classes. Maria got to class just as the bell rang, rushed to her seat, pulled out paper and pen, and began to complete the warm-up activity posted on the whiteboard. The class was quiet because everyone had to complete the activity while the teacher took the attendance. He expected all students to be engaged the minute they came into his classroom. She felt safe in this classroom because Mr. Jones seemed to be always able to detect any form of misbehavior pending and stopped it before it escalated. *Maybe the students are right that Mr. Jones has eyes in the back of his head,* she thought. How did he know when a student was not engaged or off-task while his back was turned as he wrote a problem on the board? Some students thought he was strange, but Maria respected and appreciated his brilliant mind and his ability to bring math to life. She could apply math concepts to science and understood their importance in her day-to-day life. She wished all her teachers made their subject as interesting as Mr. Jones made math.

"Miss Rodriquez, are you daydreaming again? These days you seem to be going off to a faraway land in your mind. Young lady, I expect you to be focused when you come into this classroom."

"Yes, sir, I am sorry," Maria replied. She had gotten used to Mr. Jones' way of speaking. He could come across as stern and cold, but he had a good heart and wanted the best for his students, so she did not feel offended in the least. She made up her mind to try and keep focused on all her classes; at least, she felt safe in his class. Angie would not dare to pick on her because he did not tolerate any form of disrespect and bullying in his class.

She was placed in a group with Terry and was again surprised that she cooperated and contributed to solving the problems assigned. She had been showing more interest lately and seemed to be more focused. *She could be a very nice girl if she pulled herself out of the clique,* Maria thought. Maria had two classes with Angie, math and language arts. Luckily for her, Mr. Jones never placed her in Maria's group; for that, she was grateful. The sound of the bell signaled it was time to move to her next class. Maria hoped she would not pass any of her "tormentors" on the way to her other classes. She kept reminding herself of her resolution to "keep her cool."

The walk to her language arts class was uneventful; both Angie and Brianna would be there, and that sometimes spelled trouble. As usual, they sat beside each other and disrupted the class with their continual chatter and laughter. Angie was quite disrespectful to Miss Lewis, and Brianna cheered her on with outbursts of laughter. Her behavior certainly was not funny, and some students "fed off" the negative behavior. Miss Lewis was young and fresh out of college, and this was her first teaching assignment. Maria was sorry for her because she had not yet mastered the art of classroom management. She was a good teacher, and they could learn a lot if they just took the time to listen and complete the assignments given. Both girls were failing the class, and it did not seem to bother them in the least. Brianna was short, dark, and beautiful, while Angie was tall, fair, freckled, and slim. They both had a lot in common, their character and their interests, and they were more concerned with their appearance than with their education. Brianna was a follower and jumped to do Angie's bidding whenever she "barked."

It did not appear that she was concerned with her own future. Maria tried to keep out of their way because she was always the target of their vicious tongues. Angie was the leader of the group; Maria wondered what she was like when she did not have her cheerleaders cheering her on. What would cause Angie to want to bully others?

Maria snapped back to reality; she must pay attention in class and stop spending time wondering about others. She must not get distracted. Maria had yet to decide on her career goal, so it was more important that she performed well in all her subjects and be ready for whatever path her decisions led. She knew the importance of a good GPA. She must keep her grades up if she wants a scholarship to college. Maria was pleasantly surprised that she was not the focus of the girls' jokes that day; somehow, they were rather quiet, and it appeared that they were completing the assignment.

Maria smiled to herself, thinking, *Today is going well so far; let me complete the assignment.* Halfway through the assignment, she felt a touch on her back, and a note was passed to her. She heard giggling and wondered what the joke was. She opened the note, which read, "Did you buy your jeans at Goodwill, or did you get them out of the garbage can? You are so lame. No wonder you don't have any friends." Maria was furious and hurt; she could not understand how anyone could be so cruel.

She recognized the handwriting as Angie's and wanted to respond, to get up, and punch her in the face and tell her how stupid she was. Once again, the words of her father popped into her head, and she remembered her resolution to not let anything steal her joy because her mom would be home this evening. Maria decided she would not give them the opportunity to see her react in anger or cry; she would not rise to the bait. She would demonstrate self-control and continue working. Maria chose to totally ignore them, and the giggling tapered out. She felt triumphant: she had won by deciding to ignore her "tormentors."

The bell for class change rang, and Maria hurried to her next class. As she rushed through the hallway, she thought of the new girl, Jackie, who shared three classes with her. This was her first week in school, and Maria was not sure if anyone had welcomed her. She heard footsteps behind her and turned to see Jackie hurrying to class. Jackie was tall and beautiful, with a dark complexion, a warm and friendly smile, and a confident stride. As Jackie approached, Maria stopped her, introduced herself, and suggested they walk together to class. Jackie introduced herself, and Maria asked her where she was from and what school she transferred from. Jackie shared that she had transferred there from New York.

"Oh, that's great. How do you and your parents like Florida? The climate is so different here," Maria asked.

"Oh no, I did not come to Florida with my parents. My mom died, and my dad sent me to live with my Aunt Lisa. He said he could not take care of me by himself, and I would be safer with his sister because he worked long hours, and he did not want me to be by myself when I got home. My dad works for Rigger Engineering LLC, a huge company in New York, and he is their chief engineer. He is working on a very large and important project, and he even takes work home. He wants me to stay with my aunt until the project is completed."

"How long will the project take?" Maria asked.

"Maybe a year or so."

Maria stopped in her tracks; how could she have been so insensitive? In retrospect, Jackie did not seem to have any friends; she had never seen anyone engaging or including her in any conversation. Maria felt remorseful about the situation; she was too engrossed in her own troubles to notice the new girl had no friends. How thoughtless of her. As they walked into the classroom, Maria invited Jackie to sit beside her. She would make a special effort to make Jackie feel welcome to the school and a part of the classes they shared. They sat down just as the late bell rang.

Maria could not get the thought of Jackie losing her mother and her father sending her to live with her aunt. Although she understood the situation, she knew it must have been a very difficult decision to make, and it must be hard on Jackie with her mom dying and not being able to see her dad every day. At least she still lived with Mom and could see her every day. She was more blessed than she had realized. She would no longer take anything Mom did for her for granted. It made her love and appreciate her mother more. Maria thought to herself, *I wonder how Jackie is coping emotionally and mentally with her situation. I do not know how I would handle the situation if I were in Jackie's shoes.* It made her feel selfish, and she purposed in her heart to help Jackie out in any way she could. *It would be nice to get to know her better,* she thought.

The class finished, and Maria realized that she had not paid attention. She asked Jackie if they got any homework and told her she would like to get to know her better. "Jackie, I am sorry that I did not make you feel welcome. I, too, have lost a parent; maybe we should exchange phone numbers. We both understand the trauma and pain of losing someone close to us. We have some things in common, and we could encourage each other." They walked together to their next class, talking about school in general. The rest of the day went well, and Maria was proud of herself: she had not gotten into an altercation with any of her tormentors. She was excited.

After bidding Jackie goodbye, she ran to the bus loop. She could not wait to see Mom and share with her the successes of that day and tell her about Jackie. She spent the bus ride thinking about Jackie and the challenges that she faced. *Losing her mother and then having to live with a relative must be very painful,* Maria thought. *I really need to be a friend to her and stop thinking so much about myself and my problems. At least, I live with one parent,* and that is a blessing she would no longer take for granted.

Chapter 5

"Maria, this is your stop. Aren't you going to get off the bus?"

Maria came out of her daydreaming and thanked Mr. James, the driver. Running all the way home, she was full of energy and joy because her mom would be home from the hospital. She ran through the front door shouting, "Mom, I am home," but she got no response. She ran to the kitchen, then upstairs to her mother's bedroom; Mom was nowhere in sight. It did not even appear as if her mom had come home from the hospital. Maria was disappointed and concerned at the same time.

Because she didn't meet her mother at home, Maria began to worry, wondering if something else had happened to her at the hospital while she was still there. Panic took over as she ran to the phone to call the hospital. She dialed the number of the hospital, gave them the room number, and waited for her mom to answer the phone. "Hello," the receiver answered. Maria did not recognize the voice on the other end of the line;

she asked the person if she could speak to her mother, but the lady informed her that she had the wrong room number. She was the person assigned to that room. Maria became confused and started to cry. Thoughts ran through her mind. *Where is Jamie, and why isn't he home? What has happened to my mother? Why is she not home either? Is Mom dead? Is anyone going to tell me anything?* She screamed and became hysterical, assuming the worst. She began to encourage herself. "I am overreacting; Mom maybe was held up and is on her way home. Let me call Mary to see if she is with her," she said to herself.

Maria picked up the phone and started to dial when she heard the key turning in the lock; she threw the phone down and ran, reaching the front door as it opened. It was Jamie.

"Jamie, where is Mom?" Maria screamed.

"Calm down, Maria. Mary took Mom to the pharmacy to pick up her prescription. They will be home shortly."

Maria breathed a sigh of relief that her mother was okay.

"Well, let us prepare something for her to eat," Jamie said. "She is on a special diet; we too must change the way we eat. Dad died from a heart attack, and now Mom had a scare with her heart as well. We must make sure she eats the right foods, and we must do the same. We have their genes; we may be prone to heart disease, so we must eat healthy from now on."

Maria agreed. “So, what are we going to prepare?”

“I looked at the diet plan that she got from the hospital, and it states that she should have as little red meat as possible. I think we ought to just cut it out of our diets immediately. We will focus on fish, chicken, peas, beans, lentils, whole grain products, and lots of vegetables. We also must lessen our consumption of refined products and eat fresh fruits and vegetables.”

Maria was not too happy about cutting beef out of her diet because she loved a good piece of steak. However, she had to consider her mother’s health and, ultimately, their own health. That was not too much to ask for the health of the family.

Jamie told her to prepare the place settings, and he would prepare salmon, sweet potatoes, and a salad for dinner. Both their dad and mom were great cooks, and Jamie and Maria had watched them cook on many occasions. They were encouraged to assist because their parents believed they needed such a life skill. This skill was now becoming handy because they had decided to take over the cooking so that Mom could get more rest. They worked silently, each engrossed in their own thoughts. The smell of the salmon on the grill reminded Maria that she was hungry; she quickly prepared the table, adding an extra place setting for Mary just in case she was hungry when she brought Mom back from the pharmacy, so she could have a meal with them. Her thoughts went back to the wonderful times they had as a family when her dad was alive. They both had to grow up rather quickly, and they would have to take over doing more of the tasks that their mom usually performed. She would propose to Jamie that he cook, she would do the laundry, and they could both share the house cleaning. She hurriedly completed the place settings and went into the kitchen to discuss her proposal with Jamie. Jamie thought this was a good idea, only that there would be days when he would be playing soccer and would not be able to prepare dinner in time. He proposed that whenever this happened, they would switch roles. Maria and Jamie quickly completed the dinner and put the kettle on so everyone could have some tea.

"Dinner will be ready in half an hour; by then, Mom should be home," Jamie said.

"Tomorrow, we can surprise her and make her favorite dessert, chocolate cake."

"You're right. I will be home."

Soon, they heard a car honking in the front yard. Jamie and Maria rushed to the front door to greet their mom. They were so excited to see her; they hugged her so hard that she almost fell. Jamie grabbed her bag and led her by the hand; he wanted her to sit down and rest.

"I have been resting for the last thirty hours and have spent most of that time in bed, so I can stand a little," she objected.

Jamie thanked Mary for all she had done for their mom and invited her to stay for dinner. Mary thanked him for the invitation but declined the offer saying she had to go home to prepare dinner for her family and they needed the time alone as a family. She hugged each of them and told them she would check on their mom the next day.

“I'll walk you to the car,” Jamie said. He thought this was a good opportunity to talk to Mary privately about his mother's condition. “What are the doctors really saying? Is Mom really going to be okay?”

“Yes, she is; however, she will have to change her diet, eat more fish and vegetables, less red meat, and exercise. She also must take a blood thinner for six months, and she should exercise at least four times a week. She can live a normal life. You and your sister should also change your diets because of your family history.”

Jamie promised that they would do that and shared with her the plans he and his sister had made to prepare the meals at least during the week and to help with laundry and house cleaning.

“That is thoughtful of you. Karla will surely appreciate that. It would take a huge pressure off her, and she would be able to get some rest. It is important that she gathers her strength back. I am proud of you, kids; you have surely risen to the challenge. It has not been easy, but you have demonstrated a maturity far beyond your years. I will check on Karla when you are at school. The doctor said she should take two days off. I took in the doctor's note to her two jobs, so they are aware of the situation."

"Thank you again, Mary; this would have been much more difficult if we did not have you in our lives. You are a good friend to our mom."

Jamie ran up the steps. *I better run and get that dinner out of the oven,* he thought. Maria had removed the place setting and just served Mom a cup of her favorite tea, as she always had a cup before dinner. That would give him time to put the meal into dishes and place them on the table. It was a long time that they had not sat down to eat together as a family at the table because Mom was always working to make ends meet. This was one of his favorite times of the day when Dad was alive. Mom never worked, and when Dad came home, they always ate together; this was the time they would share with each other. Mom would ask, "How was your day, Carlos?" and Dad would give a description of the day, plus the laughter and the challenges. Then she would, in turn, ask Maria and him about their day, and they would have fun laughing and talking. How he missed those times. He would treasure every moment he spent with his family from now on. Dad always said, "Tomorrow is promised to no man, so we should always make the best of every opportunity to cherish our loved ones and let them know how much they are loved." Jamie had heard his dad say these words many times, but now he understood them. Dad was gone, and he almost lost Mom too. He would ensure that he showed love and understanding to his mom and sister. Life can be short.

"Mom, I sure hope you are ready to eat because I'm going to put the dinner on the table now, and then, I'll help you to the table."

"I am not an invalid, Jamie. I can walk all by myself, but thank you for your thoughtfulness. Before we eat, we need to thank God for His faithfulness to us. He certainly had His hand on me."

They held hands at the table while Mom prayed, thanking God for His blessings, His provisions, His mercy, and His grace to them.

"Can we eat now?" Maria asked. "I am so hungry."

"Yes, let's eat while Mom fills us in on her stay in the hospital."

The children wanted to know what procedures were done and discuss the changes that, as a family, they would make to their lifestyle to avoid a repeat of their mom's problem.

"Mom, we will encourage you to keep on track by changing our diets to the foods you are required to eat. After all, we have yours and Daddy's genes, and we must be careful too. In addition, we will take turns walking and exercising with you to keep you on target. We are going to hold you accountable and ensure that you follow the doctor's instructions. We don't want to lose you, Mom," Jamie said.

"You won't lose me, honey. I plan to stay around for a very long time. I want to see you both grow up and have families of your own, to experience the love and joy that your dad and I shared as we watched you grow."

"That is more like it," Maria said. "We want you around too, Mom."

Turning to her brother, she said, "The meal is delicious, Jamie. When did you learn to cook like this? I never noticed you ever paid attention to Mom whenever she was cooking. You are a natural talent."

"Thanks, sis, you're not too bad yourself. I guess we both got the natural talent from both Mom and Dad. Remember, Dad loved to cook too. It was just that he never had much time to do so, but when he did, we always enjoyed his meal. He always said if he had not opened a flower shop, he would have opened a restaurant."

"Oh, good memories. What I enjoyed most were the times when we both would prepare a meal together. Those were special and fun times," Mom recounted. "We did have a lot of fun together, and we will make it happen again; life is too short. We must take time to, as they say, 'stop and smell the roses.'" They then fell into some dead silence, each not saying a word. This is becoming more of a habit, Maria thought. *We need to make the effort to converse more and have fun together.*

Their silence was interrupted by the ringing of the doorbell. "Are you expecting anyone, children?"

"No," they responded.

"I'll get it," Jamie said as he pushed back his chair and walked to the door. "May I help you?"

"I am looking for Mrs. Rodriquez, is this where she lives?" the visitor inquired.

"Yes."

"May I come in? I need to speak with her."

"Mom, it's a policeman. He wants to talk to you."

"That is strange, a policeman wanting to see me. I wonder what for." Karla felt as if her heart had sunk to the bottom of her feet. She felt very nervous and afraid as thoughts ran through her head. *Why would a cop come to my house? Something must have happened, but I cannot think of anything. Was someone in an accident?* Maria shifted uncomfortably in her seat as she watched the expressions of fear and confusion play across her mother's face. *Did Mom do something wrong at work, or did Jamie do something bad at school, and they did not know about it? Is he here to tell us of some tragedy?* But then again, her parents did not have any siblings, and both sets of grandparents were dead. So, it could not be a tragedy. *Is he here to arrest Mom for something she did? I know that Mom would never do anything illegal, so this must be something else.* The more Maria thought, the more nervous she felt. She snapped herself back into the moment.

The cop made his way in. Maria could see sweat breaking out on her mom's forehead. *Is this a sign of guilt? Why is Mom so nervous? Can things get any worse than they already are?*

"Good afternoon, Mrs. Rodriquez. May I speak to you in private?"

"It's okay. You can speak in front of my children."

"Are you sure you want them to be a part of this conversation? I would think you would want to discuss the matter at hand outside the ears of your children. I would strongly suggest that we speak in private."

Jamie and Maria glanced at each other, both petrified. This seemed to be a very serious matter. Maria broke down in tears.

"It's okay, Maria; there is nothing to worry about. You and your brother go upstairs while I meet with this gentleman."

"Okay, Mom, we are upstairs if you need us," Jamie replied, looking perplexed.

They went upstairs into Jamie's room. "I don't like this," Jamie said. "And what can we do if Mom needs us? We cannot call the police because he is the police."

"Mrs. Rodriquez, where were you last night?" the cop asked with a stern look.

"I was at the hospital."

"What time did you get there, and what time did you leave? Who were you visiting?"

Karla got very upset. "Can you ask me the questions one at a time?"

"You are not in charge here. I am," the cop answered.

"But you are in my home where I am in charge. If you want me to answer your questions, then I politely ask you to be respectful to me. I will answer your questions one at a time. I did not visit anyone at the hospital."

"But you said you were at the hospital, so what business did you have there?"

"I was a patient there; I went in yesterday morning by ambulance, and I was discharged this afternoon. I spent one night in the hospital. As a matter of fact, I have only been home for two hours. So, I do not know what I could have done that would cause you to pay me a visit. Officer, I am a law-abiding citizen who works two jobs to feed, house, and clothe my children. I do not have time for anything else, and it is because of that schedule that I ended up in the hospital in the first place. I am overworked and tired."

"Okay, Mrs. Rodriquez, let us start over. I guess I did 'start off on the wrong foot.' I am Officer Jones, and I am investigating a hit-and-run. A witness said they saw you hit the pedestrian, and then you sped off."

"I do not own a car. I had to sell it after my husband died. You must be mixing me up with someone else."

"Aren't you Mrs. Karlan Rodriquez?"

"No, I am not, I am Mrs. Karla Rodriquez."

"What! Let me double-check my computer. Excuse me; I'll be right back."

Maria and Jamie heard the front door open and ran down the stairs, eager to hear what had transpired. "Mom, what was all that about?" Jamie asked.

"It is a case of mistaken identity; he has gone outside to recheck the name. He will be back shortly."

The front door opened, and Officer Jones walked in looking quite sheepish. "I must apologize, ma'am, for the mix-up. You were right; you are the wrong Mrs. Rodriquez. You both have the same street address, just a different house number. I am sorry for the trauma I put you through, and I hope you get well soon."

"You have two lovely children; continue to train them right. I see too many children their age out on the streets doing drugs and getting into trouble. It is refreshing to see that your children are not a part of the problem. You are doing a good job; keep it up! I am sorry to learn about your husband's death; it must be quite a challenge raising those two children on your own. Thank you for your time and patience. I'll see myself out." He then walked out.

Karla breathed a sigh of relief. "What a day, who would believe we would get such an unlikely visitor?"

"The type of visitor that no one ever wants to have," Maria said.

"Well, at least today was not boring, stressful perhaps, but certainly not boring. I was accused of a hit-and-run. The police officer said a witness identified me as the driver. I cannot even drive, never had a license."

"That's why you hit the pedestrian, Mom, do not get behind the wheel of a car again until you learn to drive," Jamie teased. They all burst into laughter.

"Time for roll call, inmate 343, Karla Rodriquez," Jamie laughed. It was fun to joke around; their mom would never get around the wheel of a car without a license.

"Time for bed," Mom said. "You'd be up early in the morning for school. I'll be sleeping in and getting some needed rest."

"We'll be up early and prepare breakfast and lunch for you, Mom, and when we get home, we will prepare dinner, so take the opportunity to relax. We got it all covered."

"Thank you, children, and have a good night."

They ran over, embraced and kissed their mom, and made their way up to bed. "I'll be up shortly," Mom added. "I am just taking some time to unwind and reflect on God's goodness and mercy."

Chapter 6

Maria was tired and fell asleep as soon as her head touched the pillow. It did not seem as if she was asleep for long when she was awakened by the sound of breakfast dishes. Jamie must have gotten up early and started breakfast. She couldn't understand why he did not wake her, so she could help him. She glanced at the clock, and it was 6:15 a.m. "Time to get up," she said aloud to herself. She still felt tired but knew that this was not the time to stretch and that she had to take her time getting ready. She had to help Jamie, so he would not be late for school. Maria ran into the shower, then hurriedly got dressed, and went downstairs. She took over from her brother and completed the breakfast, gave Mom a cup of tea, and told her when she was ready for breakfast, she would find her meal on the table.

She sat down to eat with Jamie and told him that it was okay he could leave for school; she would take care of the dishes, prepare a sandwich and some fruits for Mom's lunch and leave them in the refrigerator. Jamie went in to say goodbye to Mom, then stopped to hug and thank Maria, then he ran through the door. She finished breakfast, did the dishes, and ran upstairs to brush her teeth. She was so happy Mom was home. It was time to go catch the bus.

"Bye, Mom, see you later. I love you. Your lunch is in the refrigerator, do not forget to have your breakfast and lunch. We want you to eat and get some rest." Maria bounded out the door and set off jogging to the bus stop, singing to herself. "Someone is happy this morning," a voice broke into her singing moment. She stopped and turned around to see who it was because she had no recollection of passing anyone. But there was no one there. By the pathway were some thick bushes, and she wondered if someone was behind the bushes. She became frightened and began to run faster, but it seemed the voice was keeping up with her.

"You are happy, and I am sad and angry. Your mother ran over my little girl, and she is dead; because of her, I will never see my little girl again. She did not even stop to help her; if she had stopped, my little girl would be alive today. Now, I am going to take your life, so she will feel the same pain I am feeling. The pain of losing her little girl."

Maria picked up her pace, but the faster she ran, the faster the person ran, and it seemed that she could not outrun him. "Who are you?" she blurted. "My mother did not run over your little girl; it was another Mrs. Rodriquez, you can ask Officer Jones."

"I do not want to hear any lies; it was your mother."

By then, Maria was panting, she felt as if she could not run any further, she could see the bus stop in the distance and already children were standing there. She tried to cry for help, but no sound came out of her parched throat. She felt that she would not be able to make it, but she kept saying to herself, "I can make it because I can do all things through Christ, who gives me strength." She had learned that verse of Scripture years ago as a little girl; now, she must exercise her faith and believe that she could outrun this man who had no face. She could not see him but could hear him running on the other side of the bushes, out of sight. She could not tell anyone about it because no one would believe her; the children at the bus stop would not see the man chasing her. Everyone would think she was crazy. He was not chasing her but running beside her out of sight. As Maria got closer to the bus stop, the footsteps petered out, and there was no sound of the footsteps again. She stopped and bent over to catch her breath, glad she had escaped but wondering who it was and if the faceless man would really try to kill her. She couldn't believe this was happening to her, as it seemed surreal, like it was a nightmare.

Maria jumped up out of her sleep. Someone was shaking her by the shoulders and calling her name.

"What's wrong? I could hear you gasping for breath. Are you alright?" Jamie asked.

"You mean this was really a dream? I did not get dressed, eat, run to the bus stop, and was chased by a man? Oh, thank God it was not real. In my dream, someone was chasing me, telling me that they were going to kill me because Mom had run over their little girl, and now, she was dead. I guess what you heard was me running and gasping in my sleep. I really feel that I have been running."

"It's okay, Pumpkin; it was only a nightmare."

"But why would I have this dream?"

"Because of all the trauma we have been through lately and your fear of losing Mom."

"I hope I never have a dream like that again. So, we did not make breakfast, and you did not leave for school."

"No, all that was part of your dream, but it is time to get up now. I will fix breakfast and lunch for Mom. Take your time and gather yourself, get ready, and come down for breakfast. I will not allow anyone to harm you. I am your big brother, I love you, and I will take care of you and Mom. So, don't worry that pretty head of yours."

Maria was grateful that she had a brother that loved her; she felt safe when he was around, more like the same feeling she had when her dad was around. She thought, *I guess he has taken over Dad's role. He is such a good brother.*

"Breakfast is ready!"

She could hear Jamie's voice floating up the stairs. "I will be down in a second," she responded. No time to waste fixing her hair any better than it was; she had a hard time putting her unruly hair up, something she inherited from her father. How she wished she had hair like her mom. Mom's hair styled easily and was always well-groomed. She had gotten up late and, if she did not hurry, she would be late for school. She ran into her mother's room. She was having the cup of tea Jamie had given her. Maria gave her a kiss, ran down the stairs, and quickly ate her breakfast. Within fifteen minutes, she had finished her breakfast, brushed her teeth, ran in to tell Mom goodbye, and was out the door.

Maria ran to the sidewalk and stopped suddenly as a surge of fear grasped her when she recalled the nightmare she had. She reminded herself that it was only a dream, and this would not happen to her in real life. She began to speak to herself, "Be brave, do not be afraid; there is nothing to fear but fear itself." That was something Dad had often told her when, as a little girl, she was fearful of the dark. She heard herself saying, "God has not given me a spirit of fear but of power, love, and a sound mind." She learned that verse of Scripture from her mom. She kept talking to herself as she made her way slowly to the bus stop. She wished her friend John were on the bus; she really needed to talk to him.

Maria slowed down her pace; she did not want to be standing at the bus stop too long just in case Terry was on the bus and decided to torment her. She could not promise anyone that if she were ridiculed by one of those girls, she would not retaliate. She was aware that her hair was not combed the way she liked it because she had run out of time. But if John was on the bus, then Terry dared not say anything negative to her. She continued at a slow pace, willing herself to be positive, not to anticipate the negatives and the what-ifs. It did not make sense thinking about potential problems that did not exist. *Why should I anticipate a bad day at school? It will be a good day today. Mom is okay, she is home, and nothing or no one can take away my joy. I will keep in mind that "a soft answer turneth away wrath, but grievous words stir up anger." I refuse to get angry today because I once read that whoever causes me to lose my cool or to get angry controls me, and no one controls me. I will succeed,* she encouraged herself.

Suddenly, she became aware of someone walking behind her, and she glanced around to see if it was someone from her school, but it was not; she did not recognize the man who was walking a few steps behind her. She picked up her pace as she remembered her dream. *This could not be happening; my dream could not become reality,* she thought. The footsteps also seemed to be going faster to match her steps.

She began to panic, then the man behind called out to her, "Why are you afraid? Did your mom think about my little girl after she hit her? Did she ever consider that she was hurt and scared? I do not think so because she kept driving. Now she is going to feel what I am feeling. I will make sure of that; never consider yourself safe. I will make her life a living nightmare."

"My mom did not hit your little girl; it was another Mrs. Rodriquez." Maria tried to scream as she began to run. The man also began running.

"Tell your mother I am after her family."

Maria wondered if she had somehow gone back to bed and was reliving the same dream. But this felt so real, just as that other dream felt. She pinched herself, and it hurt. Then, she became aware that she no longer heard footsteps following her; she glanced around, no one was there. "Am I imagining things?" she asked herself. She slowed her pace down and began to repeat to herself, "I do not have a spirit of fear, but of power, love, and a sound mind."

"That is my girl," John said as he approached her. She had not realized that she was talking out loud. Anyone hearing her would think she was crazy. *Only crazy people talk to themselves,* she thought. She tried very hard to be calm, as she did not want to share her dream and what had just happened with John while they were standing at the bus stop. She did not want anyone to overhear what she had to tell John. She looked around and spotted Terry standing not too far from them. "I am so glad to see you, John. I have so much to tell you, but I will wait until we are seated on the bus." They could see the bus in the distance and as it pulled in at the stop. John and Maria jumped on and found seats together.

"John, I know if you are on the bus with me, I will be safe from rude comments. I cannot thank your mother enough for being there for Mom. She surely is a real friend to her; it took a lot of the pressure off Jamie and me. You would never guess what happened to us after your mom left. I still cannot believe it, I was so frightened, but I am happy that everything is alright now." Maria proceeded to bring John up to date on the visit from Officer Jones. John could not believe his ears. Could the police make such a big blunder? She also shared with him her dream and what had just happened to her on her way to the bus stop and explained to him that it was why she was talking to herself.

"I was encouraging myself, and it made me feel better."

"I am glad that is behind you and your mother is back home. I cannot begin to imagine being in your shoes. You've been a trouper. I will certainly look out for you at school more. You can depend on me, like a big brother."

"Thank you, John."

The bus rolled into the bus loop, they got off the bus together, John gave her a hug, and they separated for classes. It dawned on her that she never even gave Terry and her friends a thought; she had bigger problems on her mind.

Maria linked up with the new girl Jackie. She was not yet comfortable with her to tell her anything about her family, but she had decided to make her feel welcome and be a friend to her, and that was what she would do. They both walked to math class getting there just as the first bell rang. They took their seats and proceeded to complete the math problems on the board. Mr. Jones rarely placed two problems on the board, but today he did. *I wonder why,* Maria asked herself as she settled down to work the problems. Jackie was pretty good at math herself. Maria believed that Mr. Jones would soon ask her to lead one of the groups. That would free him up more to move around each group as they worked on new concepts. She hoped that Jackie would not become a target because of her friendship with her. But then again, Jackie seemed to be able to take care of herself, she did not look as if she was afraid of anyone, and she did not care what anyone thought about her. She had picked this up from the little conversations she had with her during the week. Maybe eventually they could exchange numbers, but it was too early for that—they did not know each other well enough. Her thoughts were interrupted by the ringing of the late bell. She had already completed the assignment on the whiteboard and decided to read the topic that would be covered during class.

Mr. Jones called on Jackie to go to the whiteboard and work one of the problems. The class was impressed by Jackie's math ability and the simple way in which she explained each step. It made the problem look quite easy. Even someone who was "dumb" at math could understand. She was now positive that Jackie would be a good choice to lead one of the groups. But then, that would be Mr. Jones' decision to make. "Terry, will you go to the board and work the other problem?" he asked.

The air was charged with silence. It seemed everyone held their breath. The class knew that Terry was not very good at math, and most of the time, she did not pay attention. Mr. Jones was known to call on students who were not engaged in the activity he had given. Maria felt compassion for Terry because she knew Mr. Jones would not be pleased if she worked the problem incorrectly. She assumed he made Jackie go first because he knew Jackie's ability and felt that Jackie would be able to present the material in a way everyone could understand. Terry timidly walked to the board, took up the dry erase marker, and began to work the problem. So far, so good, she attempted to explain what she was doing, but it did not come across quite clearly. The important thing is that she completed the problem correctly. The class burst out clapping, for it was the first time Terry had gone up to the board and solved a math question correctly.

Mr. Jones banged on the desk and said, "This is not a concert; why are you clapping? I expect all my students to do well. Congratulations, Miss Bell, you have done a good job. Keep it up."

Terry's face lit up with excitement, "Thank you, sir."

Jackie had explained the solution to the previous problem in such a way that she understood. She must thank Jackie at the end of the class.

Angie was looking angry and upset. She was not good at math and never listened in class. But she always felt okay in class because she hung out with Terry, who hated math as much as she did. If she had company, she did not feel too bad, but Terry had to go and spoil it for her. Now Angie felt she would look stupid as the only one who was not able to work a math problem correctly. As Terry walked to her desk and sat down, she heard Angie whisper in her ears, "You just had to go up there and show off. I guess you think you are a math genius now. Solving one math problem does not make you a genius."

Terry felt deflated. This was her friend, and she assumed that Angie would be happy for her; instead, she insulted her. Maria listened to the quiet interchange; she could hear the anger in Angie's voice. Now the tables were turned, and Terry was on the receiving end of Angie's anger. This was an interesting development in Maria's view. She wondered how this would play out if they should turn on each other. Maria felt sorry for both; all this time, Terry had pretended to be "dumb" because she did not like math. Maria was glad Terry listened in class that day and tried to understand, and now she would see that math is not too bad after all.

The bell went, and everyone gathered their belongings and rushed to their next class. Jackie waited for Maria, so they could walk together to the next class. "You explained the math problem well, such that Terry could understand. She has never solved a math problem in class before. Thanks to you, she was able to follow the steps and explanations you gave and use that knowledge to solve the assigned math problem."

"I'm glad I was able to help. I love math, and it comes easily to me."

"That makes two of us," Maria agreed. "The only thing is, I am not able to explain as well as you do. Good job."

"I am sure you are better at other things than I am," Jackie responded. "Let us hurry to class before the late bell rings."

The rest of the day went well. Maria said goodbye to Jackie and ran to catch her bus. John was taking the bus as well. It was not very often that he took the bus both ways, but Maria was happy about that because it meant she would have an uneventful ride home. She would be sitting beside her best friend, so she would not be anyone's target today. They sat down.

"How was your day?" John asked.

"Quite interesting," Maria proceeded to tell John about the disagreement between the two friends, Angie and Terry. "I am only happy that I was not on the receiving end of their tongue today. I wonder if this will affect their friendship. Terry is not a bad person; she is only following the other three, Angie, Brianna, and Lori. I hope she will pull out of the group and find out she is quite a smart girl."

"I hope she does," he responded with a shrug.

The bus pulled up to their stop, and they came off.

"I'll walk you home," John offered. "I have been thinking of what you told me about your dream this morning and how you felt as you walked to the stop. And that on the way to the bus stop, you experienced a similar situation to your dream. If you do not mind, I will share this with my mother and see if I could take the bus with you to and from school until you feel more confident and comfortable. I do not want you to be crippled by fear. We'll talk about this more; I will call you later to let you know if my mother agrees with my plan."

"Thank you so much, John; I do appreciate your thoughtfulness. This would certainly make me feel better, and I do hope your mother will agree. I will work on my fears, so you don't have to keep doing this for a long period of time."

They walked leisurely to the door, and John asked if he could come in and say hi to Mrs. Rodriquez. He had not seen her since she went into the hospital.

"Sure, I am sure my mother will be happy to see you." She led him in. "Mom, I am home, and I have a visitor for you. Can we come up?"

"I was just about to come downstairs. Jamie came home earlier, and I could hear him in the kitchen preparing dinner," she answered as she came down the stairs.

"Your mom sounds energetic in her voice. She seems well."

"God's intervention at work, I must say."

Her face brightened up when she saw John. "Oh, John, it's you! What a pleasant surprise. I see you walked my daughter home from the bus stop; thank you."

"Yes, ma'am, I did. She encountered some challenges this morning, so I've decided to meet her here in the mornings; we would walk together to the bus stop, and I would walk her from the bus stop in the evenings. I will walk her home until she feels comfortable walking home by herself."

"What incident, Maria?"

"I'll tell you all about the incident later, Mom."

John went further, saying, "My mom told me about your hospitalization, and I decided to take the opportunity to visit with you to see how you were doing. I hope you are feeling much better and will be back to normal soon."

"Thank you. I don't know what I would have done without your mother and the children. Have a seat, John. I want you to tell me what challenges Maria faced this morning."

"I would prefer if Maria told you herself, Mrs. Rodriquez."

Maria shared what she had experienced on her way to the bus stop.

"That is one reason why I decided to escort her to and from the bus stop each day," John said. "The other reason is, you see, I did not tell Maria this because I did not want her to think about this during the day, but I was at the bus stop before her, and I did see a man following her this morning. I saw her pick up her pace and, from where I was standing, he did seem to pick up his pace as well. So, it was not her imagination, her dream or at least part of it had come true."

Maria was dumbfounded; she began to panic, but John reminded her calmly that he would walk her to and from the bus stop to ensure nothing bad happened to her.

Karla was trying to be calm; she did not want Maria to see how worried she was over the incident that had taken place that morning. "Alright, John. Thanks for sharing. Jamie is cooking in the kitchen. Would you like to stay for dinner?"

"It smells delicious, and I would love to. Thanks for the invitation, but I can't stay any longer because I promised Dad I would help him work on his car this evening. He should be waiting for me, but he will be okay when I tell him I walked Maria home." He stood and then headed for the door.

"My regards to your mom and dad, John," said Mrs. Rodriquez.

"Will do, ma'am." With a thumb-up and a soft smile, he said to Maria, "Have a great weekend; and see you on Sunday. I'll ask Mom about riding the bus to and from school and let you know her answer."

"Thank you again, John; you are such a good friend. See you on Sunday."

Chapter 7

"How was your day, Maria? Would you like to tell me what incident John was talking about?" Jamie had overheard his mother's words and came bounding out of the kitchen. "Are those girls still bothering you?"

"No, Jamie, you don't understand. It was not at school; they had nothing to do with it." Maria related to Jamie what had happened as she walked to school that morning and what John had suggested doing on the matter.

"This is critical. Why didn't you report this to the school?"

She sighed and said, "I don't understand all this."

"Well, we must get in touch with Officer Jones at once and let him deal with it. Obviously, no one had updated the father of the girl. He somehow got my name and thinks I am responsible for his little girl's death," Mom said. "I hope he doesn't get himself in any trouble. Killing someone will not bring his little girl back; it will only cause more grief for the family. My heart goes out to him; I can't imagine how I would feel if I lose you or Jamie."

"Apart from that scare on my way to the bus stop, my day went well, Mom. There is a new girl at school, and her name is Jackie, she is originally from New York. We seem to have a lot in common. Her mother died, and her father sent her here to live with her aunt for a year. He is concerned for her safety. You see, he is an engineer, and he is working on a very important project that keeps him at work late at nights, and Jackie would be home alone after school."

"So, until the project is completed, Jackie will live with her aunt, and unlike me, she has no siblings. Life would be tougher for me if I did not have Jamie. It is so sad; it is like losing both your parents at once. I am grateful that I have you and Jamie. I cannot imagine how I would have felt if you had sent us away to live with someone else. Thank you, Mom; I love you more for that."

"You're welcome, honey; I would not have it any other way. I will call the police station to lodge a complaint about the threats you received from the man who said he was the father of the victim from the hit-and-run accident. My heart aches for him; I cannot imagine what he and his family must be going through. But I must protect you; this is my responsibility."

Mrs. Rodriquez proceeded to make the phone call. An officer answered, and she requested to speak with Officer Jones. The police officer informed her that Officer Jones was not in office, but if it were an emergency, she could put her on to another officer.

"Thank you, but I would prefer to speak with Officer Jones. May I leave a message for him?"

"Yes, ma'am."

"Tell him that Mrs. Karla Rodriquez called, and it is very important that he gets in touch with me as soon as possible."

"Okay, I will."

"Thank you very much! I'll look forward to his call." She hung up and turned to her children, "Well, we will just have to wait on his call."

Maria felt her stomach growling and realized that she was hungry. "Jamie, is dinner ready yet? I am so very hungry."

"In a minute, set the place settings, and dinner will be served by the time you complete setting the table. I am just finished chopping up the vegetables for the salad, and then dinner will be served."

"Good, my stomach will be very grateful."

Mom laughed, "I am a bit hungry myself. Thank you, Jamie. I feel so much better having had the opportunity to rest. I do not know the last time I have felt this energized. That food smells good, and I cannot wait to taste it. You are a good cook, Jamie."

"Thank you, Mom; I learned from the best." He left for the kitchen and soon got the food ready. "Are you finished setting the table? I am about to bring out the food."

"Almost there," Maria replied. "Bring them on."

Jamie had prepared roasted chicken, tossed salad, and a potato salad.

"This dinner is fit for a king," Mom said.

"You really outdid yourself. I cannot believe you are such a good cook. I don't remember ever teaching you to cook."

"You did not, but remember I spent a lot of time in the kitchen watching you cook, and Dad taught me a trick or two. He always invited me to join him in the kitchen whenever he was cooking. He would show me how to chop and dice and season, and he explained the steps he took in the preparation process. So, you see, Mom, I learned from both you and Dad indirectly and directly. I guess I must have inherited the love for cooking from both of you. Plus, I love to eat. I wonder who I got that trait from."

Maria burst out laughing, "We all love to eat, but we have to be careful to change the way we cook and eat fewer fatty foods."

"But a treat occasionally will not harm us," Maria opined.

The laughter was interrupted by the ringing of the telephone. *This must be Officer Jones,* Mom thought. "Jamie, could you pass me the phone, please?"

"Okay, Mom."

It was Mary calling to check up on Karla. She also wanted to hear about Maria's encounter with the stranger on her way to the bus stop. Karla went through the whole process of reporting what had happened. "Tell Maria she should be careful, and I have given John permission to walk her to and from the bus stop."

"Thanks for being there for me and my family, Mary. I really appreciate it!"

"I'll be over in the morning to check up on you. So, sleep well, and I'll see you tomorrow."

"Thank you, Mary." She hung up. "Mary and her family are good friends to us. I am glad we met; they have really stood by us throughout our challenges. You know you have a good friend when they are there for you every step of the way. Some friends will stick with you in adversity for a season, then they get tired of you and your problems and move on. But true friends never give up on you, they encourage, support, admonish, and stick with you for as long as it takes for your wounds to heal, and they are with you to celebrate your successes. I hope my children will prove themselves to be true friends too. Children, if you want a good friend, be a good friend."

Maria reacted, saying, "Thanks, Mom, I needed to hear those words; I will try my best to be a good friend. I know what I need to do where Jackie is concerned. She needs a true friend. I also think that Terry will need a good friend too. She had a run-in with Angie because she worked a math problem correctly. I really think Terry wants out of that clique; she is smart, but she is dumbing down herself to fit in with those girls. I feel bad for her. I hope she has the courage to move on out of that group. I will seek a way to encourage her, and maybe she could start hanging out with Jackie and me. I'll run that by Jackie and see what she thinks."

"That's so thoughtful and kind of you, Maria," Jamie said. "I am proud of you, little sis."

They were interrupted by the ringing of the doorbell. "I'll get it," Jamie said.

It was Officer Jones. "I got your message, Mrs. Rodriquez. I am sorry for disturbing your dinner. I was driving through your neighborhood on my way home when I got the message, so I thought it would be better if I stopped by to hear what you have to say. But I can call you later or come back another time since you and your family are at dinner."

"That's okay, Officer Jones. Would you like to join us for dinner? We have plenty of food."

"Are you sure I'm not imposing on your family time?"

"No, you are not. Sit down, please; the kids will set you a place setting."

"Thank you, ma'am; I do appreciate it. I was going to stop and pick up something to eat on my way home, but nothing beats a home-cooked meal. I have not had a good home-cooked meal since my wife died three years ago."

"Oh dear, I'm sorry to hear that. Do you have any children?"

"No, ma'am, my wife died in childbirth, and the baby died too."

"That must have been traumatic for you."

"Yes, it was. I did not think that I would ever get over it, but I had good support from a friend and colleague of mine, Officer Hugh McKenzie, who helped me through a very dark, deep, and depressive period of my life. I am very grateful to him; I do not know how I would have survived without his support. But enough about me. What is it you wanted to talk to me about?"

Karla asked Maria to tell Officer Jones her story. Maria related the story as Officer Jones took notes and asked questions. "I will visit the gentleman and inform him of his mistake. I understand his grief, but he must understand he cannot take matters into his own hands. In addition, had he followed through with his threat, he would have caused grief to an innocent family. I am sorry about that, and I will deal with the situation for you. You should not have any more problems walking to school."

Maria wanted to know what it was like being a police officer. As they continued eating, Officer Jones told them many humorous stories of run-ins with criminals and the many outrageous explanations they sometimes gave as to why they were at a specific location. Before they all knew it, it was 9 p.m. The time had passed so quickly. He thanked the family for their hospitality, complimented Jamie on his cooking, and told them he would be in touch to update them on the case, and he walked out the door.

"Mom, I think he likes you," Maria said.

"Nonsense, I barely know the man."

"It doesn't mean that you won't get to know him; he seems like a nice person."

"Well, I'm not interested. No one could ever replace your father; he was one of a kind. I would appreciate it if you never make those suggestions again."

"Yes, Mom, I just thought that maybe you needed someone to take care of you because we will grow up soon and not live with you anymore."

"You have no need to worry about me. When the time comes, I'll deal with it."

"Okay, Mom, but it does not hurt to have an open mind."

"Young lady, I think you have not heard me; the matter is not up for discussion. Understood?"

"Yes, Mom."

Jamie kept silent and didn't say anything during their exchange of words. "Let's get the kitchen cleaned up and get to bed; it is almost 10 p.m." Jamie and Maria worked in silence to clean up the kitchen. Then Maria spoke under her breath, "It was a good evening spoiled by my interference."

"Well, you meant good, Pumpkin, but Mom is right: she barely knows the man, he seems nice, but we don't know him like that. Let things be; if it is in the will of God for Mom, it will happen."

"I guess you are right. It seems Mom is yet to come to grips with Daddy's passing, so it is hard for her to even consider someone in his place. Her heart is still locked away. I will always love my daddy, and I would never consider anyone taking his place—no one can. It does not mean I would not be happy for Mom to marry again; I do not see it as a replacement of Dad. I would see it as a welcome addition to the family. Good night, Jamie; I am going upstairs to bed. I will peek in on Mom and tell her goodnight. See you in the morning."

"Sweet dreams, lil sis."

Chapter 8

Maria lay in bed reflecting on the activities and experiences of the day. She was glad Officer Jones would take care of the incident. Her thoughts went out to the unknown man who was grieving for his daughter. She deemed it apt to find out the man's name. Was she an only child, or did the little girl have siblings? If she did, how were they dealing with the tragedy in their life? Maria knew only too well the feelings of despair, hopelessness, numbness, disbelief, and pain that losing a loved one brought to one's life, especially when the death was unexpected. She felt sad for the family. She thought of getting to know more about the family.

She also wondered if Officer Jones would be able to tell her about them. Did they have any other children? If they did, she would like to help them through the grieving process, having been there herself. Well, it would not really be the same since she lost her dad, and they lost a daughter, and the kids would have lost a sister. A loved one was lost, and the pain would just be as overwhelming. She decided she would tell Mom if she could find out from Officer Jones more about the family and ask him if it would be okay for him to introduce her to them. *I know that they must go through the grieving process as I did but having someone who understood and would listen to them should make a difference,* she thought. The pain would not be any less, but her being there for them and sharing her own feelings of helplessness and the emotions that went along with grief might just help to shorten the grieving process. This would hopefully bring them closer to accepting the tragedy and begin the healing process.

Maria had no idea when she fell asleep, but she woke up feeling refreshed. She glanced at the clock and panicked; it was already 8 a.m. *I am late for school, why did the alarm not go off? Is Jamie gone to school, or is he still sleeping?* She hopped out of bed in a panic, then fell back on the bed laughing. It was Saturday; no wonder the alarm did not go off. *I had better get out of bed, make a cup of tea, and take it up to Mom. She would want a cup of tea before breakfast.* She got dressed and went downstairs only to find her mother sitting at the table sipping a cup of tea.

"Oh, Mom, I'm sorry. I had planned to be up early, but I overslept. I fell asleep late because I had so much on my mind. I kept thinking about the family who lost their daughter and wondering how they were coping with the grief. It brought back memories of when Dad had just died. I have no clue as to the time I fell asleep."

"That's okay, Pumpkin. I am feeling much better and decided to allow you, children, to sleep in. I can make myself a cup of tea; I have even decided that I would make breakfast for us, or, if you care to join me, we can make it together."

"Oh, that would be nice," Maria exclaimed. "This would feel more like old times, with us doing things together. We never cooked together before, so this will be fun. I am eleven years old, in sixth grade, and I should be able to make a nutritious breakfast. The days of babying me are over, Mom, and I insist that I take on more of the responsibilities in the house. Jamie and I have already discussed sharing some of the chores that we will take over from you, and we will not take any resistance or excuses from you."

"Okay, dear, but I will do my part and assist whenever I can."

They laughed together as they got up from the table and headed to the kitchen. Jamie emerged from his room. "What's so funny? I could hear you talking and laughing from my bedroom. Can someone not get a chance to sleep in without interference?" He laughed and then apologized, "Sorry, Mom, I overslept. I laid awake last night thinking of the events of the past couple of days."

"That makes three of us," Mom chuckled. "Things around here have become pretty interesting."

"It certainly has," Jamie agreed. "I think things are slowly returning to normalcy, though." Maria took the opportunity to share with them her idea of getting to know the family of the little girl that was killed and her plans to help them through the grieving process if they had a daughter and would allow her to.

"That is a great idea," Jamie said. "I remember how I felt when Dad died: I did not feel anyone understood the pain we were going through; they said they did, but how could they if they had never lost a loved one? If they have a son, I too would like to join Maria in this plan. I certainly hope Officer Jones will suggest it to the dad, and the family will be willing to accept the help. So, Mom, will you call him and find out if he will talk with the family?"

"I will call him and let you know what he says."

"Thank you, Mom. Let us get on with breakfast because I am starving," Maria laughed.

After breakfast, Karla called and spoke with Officer Jones, who thought it was a great idea. He informed her that the family did have a son and a daughter about the ages of her children and that he had visited with the family and made them aware of the mistaken identity. Also, he spoke with the father about him stalking Maria and explained to him the charges that could be filed against him if he continued to do so or if he chose to hurt anyone affiliated with the woman who ran his little girl over. He also explained to him how much this would hurt his family if he found himself in jail because of revenge, and revenge would never bring his daughter back. He would revisit the family to ask them if they would accept the Rodriquez family's assistance in helping them through the grieving process and get back to them with the family's decision.

By eleven o'clock, Officer Jones called to say the family had agreed to accept the help and felt it would be good to speak with people who understood what they were going through. He informed Karla that the father had apologized for his actions against Maria yesterday.

"Do you know the names of the parents and children in the family? It would be good for us to learn their names before we visit. Also, it may be best if I could speak to the parents on the phone, so we know a little bit about each other before we visit. At that time, we could set up the time for the visit."

"That is a good idea. The father's name is Jack Thomas. Mrs. Rodriquez, is it okay for me to give them your number and have them call you?"

"Certainly, thank you for your help."

"I fully understand, I have had to deal with the unexpected loss of my wife and child, and I completely understand what it means to grieve, waking every day thinking it is a dream. I think you will be hearing from the family soon."

Karla and Maria spent the rest of the morning cleaning the house while Jamie mowed the lawn and watered the flowers. After Saturday morning chores were finished, Mom suggested they go for a walk in the park to unwind and relax after such a hectic and eventful week. Nature had a way of soothing their minds. They could walk along the jogging trail, which was shaded by a variety of trees, and, usually, several species of birds could be seen nesting in the branches. She reminded Jamie and Maria of the times when Dad would play the game of identifying the birds based on their singing. Those were fun times. It was a lesson in nature. They all agreed that this would be a nice way to finish the day. She also suggested they pack some food for the picnic.

Soon, they all got ready, grabbed their picnic basket, and headed out the door. They were stopped by the ringing of the phone. "Bad timing," Mom said. "However, wait here while I answer the phone." It was the man whose daughter had died. He introduced himself as Jack; his wife's name was Susan, and they had a fifteen-year-old son, Chris, a twelve-year-old daughter, Lori, and his little daughter's name was Joanna, who was six years old. Karla offered Jack their condolences and told him a little bit about their family. They agreed her family would visit Jack and his family on Sunday at 4 p.m. Jack had given her his address as 2500 Mango Lane. It was on the next street over from their street, just a few blocks from their home. This would be an easy walk; they needed the exercise anyway, she thought.

Karla filled the children in on the details of the conversation as they walked towards the park. "Let us head for a picnic table; we are all hungry after all the work we did at home. We will eat before we take the walk," Jamie suggested and led them to the perfect table under a shed that would shade them from the sun. There was a soft wind blowing. Maria could feel the wind caressing her face; it blew gently, causing her hair to move in the wind. This added to their comfort because they would be shaded from the sun, and the gentle wind would keep them cool. As they started eating, Jamie drew their attention to a family of four walking towards them in the distance; they thought the family was there for their picnic too. As they drew closer, Maria said, "They seem so sad, everyone appears to be locked away in their own world, no joy in their eyes, 'no pep to their step.' I wonder what could make them so sad?" "Stop staring at those people; it is rude to stare," Mom said.

As the family walked past, Maria whispered, "Mom, I think I know the girl. That looks like Lori, one of the girls that I have problems with at my school. She is one of the girls from the clique that give me a hard time. But then again, maybe it is not; her face is partially covered by a hood. She is in my math class. Come to think of it, and I have not seen her in class since last week. Funny if that was really her, and I should see her out here; maybe she lives close by."

"Let us stop watching other people and eat so we can go for a walk on the trail. I long to hear the birds again; maybe we can find a seat under the trees and birdwatch."

"That'd be great, Mom; it would feel like old times, only Dad is not here," said Jamie.

Maria watched as her mom's eyes filled with tears. It was obvious that Mom was still grieving. It was not that Maria had gotten over her father's death, but she was accepting the fact that she would never see her dad again, and she could talk about it without bursting into tears. *I really miss my daddy, but life goes on, and I have a lot to be grateful for,* she would always say to herself.

They finished eating in silence, each reminiscing on old times. "If anyone were to see us now, they would say the same thing about us that we said about the family that just passed by," Jamie broke the silence. "Let us clear the table and take that walk; nature has a way of soothing our souls and making us feel peaceful. We can look for a seat and try to identify the type of birds by their songs."

Maria responded, "You are right, Jamie. It would be fun to see which one of us wins this competition."

They quickly packed the picnic basket, tossed the trash in the garbage can, and hurried to find a seat where several birds were resting in the trees above. It was springtime, and they could hear the chirping of other birds in the distance; some were flying around, others were nesting in the trees, and still, others seemed to be playing a game of chase. They seemed so happy and carefree now that the long cool winter had gone. They walked past a man and his daughter feeding the birds; it was fun to watch the birds swoop down to pick up pieces of bread in their beaks. Ducks were swimming in the pond, and there was a bustle of activity as insects, lizards, and bees moved between flowers and scrubs. The park was alive with activity. Maria burst out singing, "It's springtime in the air." Spring is a happy time of the year; it is budding with life. "Let us just walk through the park, enjoy the scenery, and get some much-needed exercise. Is that okay with you, Mom?" asked Maria.

"Yes, that is a good idea; we can go bird watching another time. For now, let us just enjoy nature and each other."

They spent the rest of the afternoon laughing, talking, and pointing out interesting sights. Before they knew it, it was time to go. "Time flies by quickly when we are enjoying ourselves. I cannot believe it is almost 5:30 p.m. Kids, it is time to head home. I surely enjoyed myself."

"Did we?" the children chimed in. "We should do this more often."

"It gives us a chance to spend time with each other doing what everyone loves," replied Mom. Nature walks were one thing the family enjoyed, and they had not had the opportunity to do this since the tragedy. It seemed that losing Dad was getting less painful for her and Jamie; at least it appeared that way to Maria, but she was not so sure about her mother. Mom was still having a very difficult time adjusting to life without Dad. There were times she had seen her crying, and when she saw Maria, she had pretended she had the "sniffles," but Maria was not fooled; she had seen those faraway looks in her mom's eyes. In those times, Dad was on her mind. But today, she seemed to have had a very good time; it was almost like old times. Her mom must have thought about her dad, but her eyes did not appear to be sad, as they were laughing, and she was having fun. Tomorrow is another day, and Maria wondered how things would go when they met with the Thomas family.

Chapter 9

Maria woke up to the sound of someone moving around downstairs. She glanced at her clock and saw that it was only two in the morning. Who could be awake at this time of the morning? It was unlike Mom or Jamie to be up at that time. *Maybe one of them could not sleep,* she thought. In a bid to find out what was happening, Maria crept slowly down the stairs trying to make as little noise as possible, so she would not disturb anyone. She could hear faint noises coming from the family room, so she headed in that direction. There was no light on, so whoever was in there was moving around in the dark. She paused. What if it were an intruder? How would she defend herself? She wanted to bolt up the stairs to Jamie, but she felt afraid to do so; she did not want to bring any attention to herself. *I am so stupid,* she thought. *I should have checked on Mom and Jamie's room first before I headed down the stairs; now, I am stuck. Oh, if I could just get to the bottom of the stairs, I could grab Jamie's hockey stick just in case I needed it. He had left it leaning against the closet by the foot of the stairs.*

She moved stealthily in the dark; she could see a faint glimmer of light from the night light in the family room. That should be enough light for her to see exactly where the hockey stick was, so she would not bump into it and make a sound. Maria got to the bottom of the steps and quickly grabbed hold of the hockey stick, reminding herself not to make a sound. She crept gingerly towards the family room. Maria froze, as there was a loud thud as if something had fallen from the mantle. The place grew eerily quiet. She stood still, not wanting to move just in case this was an intruder. She could hear footsteps coming towards her; then the lights went on. "Who is it? Jamie, Mom?" screamed Maria.

"Maria, it's me," Mom replied. "I'm sorry if I startled you. I just could not sleep and decided to make myself a cup of tea and relax a little downstairs. Yesterday, for the first time since your father's death, I allowed myself to let go and just enjoy the beauty of this world. I had a wonderful time, and I decided it was time I moved on with my life. Being sad and asking myself the question, 'What if?' cannot bring your father back. I will always love and miss him, but life must go on. Your dad would have wanted it that way; plus, with me mourning for so long, I have neglected you and your brother. I need to pull myself together and begin to live again."

"Mom, you are not dead," Maria laughed.

"I know, but I was emotionally dead, and it is just as bad as being physically dead, maybe worse. Now I must pull myself together and really live for you, Jamie, and myself."

They sat in silence for a while.

"You know, Maria, the decision we made to visit the family who lost their little girl Joanna was a very good one. When we can take our minds off our own pain and reach out to someone who is hurting, it helps us in the healing process. It is therapy for us. We must focus less on our pain and transfer our energy to helping others who are going through a similar experience. A heart of love and care is a satisfied and happy heart. Let us promise ourselves that we will be grateful for our life circumstances and complain less. Life could be worse. It will be a couple of hours before daybreak, so let us go up to bed and get some sleep. Remember, be ready for church; we will be leaving at 9 a.m."

"Thanks, Mom. Rest well."

"And next time, Maria, if you hear a sound anywhere in the house during the night, please do not think you can take matters into your own hands and fight off an intruder. Check on Jamie and myself first—there is safety in numbers; plus, in doing so, we would know if we needed to call 911 or not."

"It didn't occur to me that it could be a burglar. I just got up and began creeping downstairs. I was almost at the foot of the stairs when it occurred to me that it might not be you or Jamie down there; by then, it was too late to turn back."

"Thank God it was only me, but next time, please, remember to think before you act. Off to bed now."

Jamie woke up feeling the rays of the sun playing across his face. Every time the branches of the tree outside his window swayed in the wind, the leaves would cover the sun resulting in the room getting darker. Then just as suddenly, it swayed to the other side, exposing the sun, which would enter his room and shine on his face. Sometimes, this would annoy him because the feeling of alternating dark and light would wake him up. But this morning, as he looked through his window at the beautiful sun, he felt energized, and there was a feeling of excitement. Today he would have an opportunity to help a family who had recently lost a loved one. He thought of what he would say to them and how he could help them work through their grief. *I must be there for the boy Chris; I am only a year older than he is, and the girl, Lori, is just a little older than Maria. At least both families have two things in common; age plus the loss of a loved one.*

Jamie reflected on how difficult and challenging it was to let go of the grief of losing his father and the many times he would try to be strong for Mom and Maria. In those times, he had longed to run to his room, where he could just break down and cry. But his friend Mark was always there. Mark was a good listener; he would sit and listen as Jamie reminisced about his father. His friend was always there for him, sitting, listening, and not saying a word. How he appreciated those times, the friendship, and patience that Mark displayed. Mark knew when to encourage and when to sit still and listen; he allowed him to grieve, yet he had a way of pointing him in the direction of healing by his encouraging words. Maybe they both could befriend Chris; he surely needed people his own age who understood his grief. In time he would discuss this possibility with Chris and introduce him to Mark if he so wanted, but in the meantime, he would try to be there for Chris as Mark was for him.

"Jamie, Maria, it's time to get up. If you do not hurry, we will miss the bus and be late for church," Mom shouted from her bedroom. Jamie hopped out of bed; he had to get to the bathroom before Maria did, or he would be late. She would always take the longest showers in history, doing what? He could not understand. *How long should it take someone to bathe and get dressed?* he thought. Maria seemed to hold the world record for taking the longest showers. He ran to the bathroom only to see the bathroom door closing; Maria had beat him to it.

"Hurry up, Maria, don't take too long, or you'll make us late. Make sure you are out by the time I get done having my breakfast. I will get yours and Mom's ready while I am at it. But please, do not spend the whole day in the bathroom."

"I promise you I will do my best to be out in record time," Maria responded.

"Thank you, Maria, I'll hold you to that," he chuckled.

True to her word, Maria was out even before Jamie finished his breakfast. "Thank you, sis; that was really a quick shower." They had picked up the pace, and soon they were on the way to the bus stop. The ride to church was not a long one, so they got there a few minutes before the service started. The family had not been to church in a while; although they had no close friends at church, it was good to reconnect with people they had not seen for quite a while.

Maria did not pay much attention to what was happening in the service until the pastor got up to deliver his sermon titled "Show love to your enemies," which caught her attention. He had read from Matthew 5 and chose verse 44 as his focus. "But I say unto you, Love your enemies, bless them that curse you, do good to them that hate you and pray for them that despitefully use you and persecute you" (Matthew 5:44, KJV). She wanted to hear how he would explain such a verse. Did he really expect anyone to treat someone who had hurt them with love and respect? What exactly did he mean? Her mind went back to her "persecutors" at school. *This should be a very interesting topic,* she mused. *Let us see what he has to say about this.*

Pastor Ben began by saying, "Most, if not all of us, have gone through some persecution at some point in our lives or have someone pay us back evil for good. How we react would determine the impact we have on others. It is easy for us to show love to a person who shows love to us. But the real test is how we treat someone when they have hurt us terribly, especially if they keep doing the same thing repeatedly."

"The bottom line is, how do we treat our enemies? What are we called to do when our beliefs are called into question? When we are faced with persecution or when we are bullied or picked on, do our actions reflect our deep moral convictions, or do we resort to the behavior of the world?" He continued, "I want to focus on loving our enemies."

Maria was more interested in the part that spoke about persecution and doing good to them that hate you. *But then again, she thought, your enemies would persecute you, and they would hate you, so I guess they are all tied together.* Her mind went back to the way she was ridiculed at school by the clique of four girls. Is she supposed to show them love? That did not seem possible, but then again, did it have anything to do with what Dad always told her? "A soft answer turneth away wrath, but grievous words stir up anger." Instead of listening to what Pastor Ben had to say about the topic, Maria had spent the time reflecting on all the challenges she faced at school daily. She felt a root of anger and bitterness forming in her heart, and instead of choosing to let it go, she nursed it until she became quite angry. Before she knew it, everyone was standing and singing the last song. She had allowed anger to seep into her spirit and missed hearing how to respond with kindness and how to love her enemies. If she had only listened, perhaps she would have gained some insight on how to deal with the problems she faced at school. It was time to go home. She got up and followed her mother and brother to the bus stop; she did not feel like talking.

"What's wrong?" Jamie asked.

"I am just reflecting on some situations, and I do not feel like talking about them now," Maria responded.

"It's okay; sometimes we like to be left alone to think things through, I understand that. However, if you ever feel like talking, you know we are here for you."

"Thank you, Jamie. I know I can depend on you and Mom."

It was twelve noon when they got home, and Mom reminded them that at 4 p.m. they would be visiting the family that lost the little girl. "I must stop referring to the family as the family that lost their little girl and use their names. They are the Thomases; we need to remember their names when we visit, so we can refer to them by their proper names. I will prepare dinner, go get some rest, or if you have homework, go complete it, so you won't have to do it when you get back from the visit." Jamie said he did not have much homework, and he would hurry to get it done so he could help their mom prepare the dinner. Maria had no homework but decided that she had a lot of reflecting to do. She needed to come up with strategies to deal with the unending problematic situations she faced at school.

Maria sat on her bed thinking about the message the pastor preached that morning. She had not heard most of it but the part she had heard kept playing over and over in her head. "Love those that hate you and do good to those that persecute you." Was that even possible? Could she love someone who hated her and forgive someone who did bad things to her? She gazed at the ceiling but not seeing, deep in thoughts. She reflected on the past week, thinking about Terry and the run-in she had with Angie. She felt bad for Terry and wished she would stand up for herself. How would Angie treat Terry tomorrow? Would they even sit beside each other? *I think I will reach out to her on the bus; I will strike up a conversation with her with the hope of getting to know her better. She needs a genuine friend, not one who bosses her around. Then, there was Lori, who had not been at school since Wednesday. I wonder if she has moved out of the area and gone to another school. That would be good, one less person to worry about,* she thought.

Maria could hear Mom calling her that dinner was ready, so they all could eat and get ready to visit Jack and his family. *I must have fallen asleep,* she thought. She got up and quickly went downstairs; the smell of freshly baked cake tingled her nose. Mom baked delicious cakes, and she had a knack for decorating. They quickly ate, cleared the table, and washed the dishes.

"Let me pack this cake to take with us," Mom said.

"Mom, I hope you baked more than one cake because I am so looking forward to a slice of your cake. It has been quite a while since you have baked and decorated a cake."

"Yes, I did bake two cakes because I know how much you children love my cakes."

"Thank you, Mom. I'll get a slice when we get back."

Mom placed the cake in the cake carrier, "Jamie, your job will be to carry the cake without dropping it. I remember when Dad died how kind and considerate our neighbors and friends were, they were always bringing over food and desserts, which meant I did not have to cook. That was a blessing, it gave me time to grieve, and I am so grateful. Whatever we can do for this family, we will do it."

Maria opened the door for Jamie and Karla to go through; she locked the door and jogged to catch up with them. Jack and his family lived on the next street over, which was Mango Lane. It meant they would walk two blocks south on their street June Plum Drive, then north two blocks on Mango Lane. This would be their exercise for the day. As close as this was, they had never gone down Mango Lane before. It was a quiet neighborhood with large homes and neatly manicured lawns.

"This is an upscale neighborhood; they must be rich," Jamie commented. "What is the number of the house again, Mom?"

"Two thousand five hundred, it should be the next one on the left. Here we are."

They got to the house; Mom went up the steps and rang the doorbell. They could hear footsteps approaching the door, and a middle-aged man opened the door and greeted them. "I am Jack. I guess you are Karla; this must be Jamie and Maria. Come on in and have a seat; I'll let my family know you are here."

"We brought this cake for you, it is our family's favorite cake, so I decided to bake one for your family. In times like these, we need all the help we can get."

"Thank you so much; we do appreciate it. I'll get the rest of the family."

As Jack went upstairs, Maria whispered, "Doesn't Jack look like the man who was with the family we saw in the park? If that is so, then he is Lori's father; she was with him in the park. She is one of the girls in the group that I have a problem with. I have not seen her at school since last week. No wonder they looked so sad and disconnected: they are in mourning."

"Now, Maria, don't get ahead of yourself; it may not be the same person. When Lori comes down, we will see if it is the Lori from your school," Mom said. "Let's not talk about this anymore."

It was a lovely house, immaculately kept, but it did not feel homely; it felt more like a museum. Everything looked expensive and in place; one did not get the feel of comfort. *Was there love in this house?* Maria asked herself. She dared not voice her opinions out loud because Mom would surely shut her up. She was taught not to criticize anyone, especially go to their homes and find fault. They could hear voices upstairs; to Maria, it seemed that the rest of the family did not want to come down. Eventually, Jack, Susan, and Chris came downstairs. Jack introduced his wife and son and apologized for Lori not wanting to socialize. "Lori was very close to her sister Joanna and took her death very hard. She was there when the accident happened and blames herself for not protecting her sister. She spends most of her time locked in her room crying, even refusing to eat sometimes. I am very worried; we have lost one daughter, and we surely do not want to lose another," Jack explained.

"We try to tell her it is not her fault, but she keeps saying it is. She also has bad nightmares, which she refuses to talk about. We can hear her crying out in her sleep, 'No, no, no,'" he added.

"This is hard for her," Karla responded.

"Yeah. Some people are so devastated by the tragedy that they find it hard to talk about it. We can only hope and pray that she will soon feel the need to share her feelings with someone who she can trust, perhaps someone who themselves has experienced tragedy. She could consider getting professional help, maybe a grief counselor. The school sometimes will bring one in for her."

"To her, it's a bad dream that she cannot wake up from. Give her time, Jack," Mom suggested. Karla gently encouraged the family to talk about the accident and explained that talking about the pain of her husband's sudden death was one thing that helped her to heal. "It might be different for you, but it would not hurt to try." She turned to Jack's wife, "Susan, would you like to tell us what happened, or just share how you are feeling?"

"All I know is that I want my little girl back; I keep going in her room to see if she is there, thinking that it is a bad dream that I keep waking up from. Then reality steps in, and I realize it is true, and she is never coming back. How do I cope with the grief? I am angry at the driver of the car; she left my little girl to die. No prison sentence she receives can take away my grief. Nothing can bring my little Joanna back. No one expects to lose a child, especially in such a way; this did not have to happen." Susan broke down crying. Chris got up and hugged his mother, telling her it would be okay, that they would survive the tragedy, while Jack sat head bowed low, wringing his hands as if in despair.

This family seemed to be facing a deeper crisis than the tragedy of losing Joanna, Karla thought; as Jack and Susan seemed so disconnected, it appeared that Chris was the strong one who was holding it together. If this was so, then the healing process would take longer unless this shared pain could reunite the family and draw them closer together. It was obvious to Karla that there were some deep wounds that had nothing to do with the accident, and for there to be total healing, the family must deal with all the other issues they had.

Jack could not shake the guilt he was feeling; he blamed himself for the accident. *If I had only stopped to take Joanna to school as Susan had asked, she would be alive today. How can I live through this? Is Joanna dead because of me? How could I have been so stupid? I was determined that my family would have the best of everything life had to offer and focused on being a successful banker, always seeking my bosses' approval so I could move up the corporate ladder, that I did not spend time with my family. I was never there for them, leaving early in the mornings and coming home late at night just to prove that I could be a success. Was it worth it? I lost sight of what was important in life. I put money and prestige before my family, and this has caused my little daughter's death. What good is all the money in the world when a loved one is gone?* Tears were threatening to flow, but he could not allow his family to see him like that; they would think he was weak. *I must be strong; I must not allow them to see how broken I am.* Jack was a proud man and prided himself on being tough. He did not feel so tough now; instead, he felt very vulnerable. Jack felt he could not allow his family and strangers to see how weak he was at that moment.

Jack's thoughts were interrupted by a loud banging overhead. He and Susan rushed upstairs just in time to see Lori throw her hairbrush across the room and pick up a chair as if she intended to throw it at the mirror. Jack grabbed the chair from her and hugged her, and assured her that all would be well, as he rocked her back and forth in his arms. His eyes filled with tears; it was a long time he had not held Lori in his arms.

"Why, why, why," she screamed. "Why did this have to happen to us? What have we done to deserve this? Life is not fair; why did my sister have to die? Why couldn't I have prevented this? The car did not even stop, Daddy. There was nothing I could do for her, her eyes were imploring me to help her, but I just stood there immobilized as I watched the breath being sucked out of her lifeless body. I watched her die, Daddy. The car tossed her like a rag doll, the driver never stopped to help, and she was left to die."

"Lori, don't blame yourself; there was nothing that you could have done to save your sister. It is not your fault. We will get through this together."

Susan was crying softly. Her heart ached that she would never see her baby girl again, but she had another crisis on her hands. She had another daughter who was hurting and needed her now more than ever; she needed to be strong for her. The three of them hugged; the grief was almost too much to bear. "I love you, sweetheart, and I am here for you," he whispered. It became clear to Jack that he had not told any of his children that he loved them in years and vowed to himself that he would try to show love and appreciation to his family. It had taken a tragedy to see how much he had neglected the emotional and mental wellbeing of his family.

Chris remained seated, rocking back and forth in his chair; as much as his sister needed him, he just could not pull himself out of his seat. The banging overhead and the screams of his sister shouting "why, why, why," had him paralyzed with fear, the fear of losing his other sister to grief. Lori had not been the same since the accident; she had spent most of her time in her room in silence, many times refusing to even eat. She was paralyzed by grief, and it appeared no one could get through to her. Her dad had suggested that she get professional counseling from a grief counselor, but she had refused.

Chris turned to Maria and asked, "Do you think you could help her through this grieving process? I know this is a bit different from you losing your dad. You did not have to watch him die, but it must have been traumatic for you. Death is always hard, especially when it is unexpected. You get up in the morning, taking life for granted, not thinking that day may be the last day you would see a loved one alive. Then, our world is turned upside down as life throws us an unexpected curveball, with no explanations on how to survive the heartache."

"I will be there for Lori and help her navigate through this dark period of her life. I do understand what she is going through. It will take some time for her to get through this and return to normalcy," Maria replied.

"Chris, you must be each other's biggest support and band together as a family. Share your feelings with each other and reflect on the fun times you had with Joanna. Find time to laugh at some funny things she did; this will help you all to heal," Mrs. Rodriquez said.

"I think we should leave you now, so you and your family can have some privacy. Let your parents know that we are there for them and that they can call us whenever they are in need. If it is okay with them perhaps, we can visit again when Lori is at the point where she feels she would like to talk to someone. Maria will be happy to spend some time with her, and if you feel you need Jamie to talk to, give him a call. I am available if your parents need me," Mom remarked.

"Thanks for coming by. I will certainly take you up on the offer; I need someone my age to talk to," Chris responded.

They walked a while in silence. Karla reflected on how difficult it was for her to put her grief aside and look to the wellbeing of Maria and Jamie. She understood only too well how Jack and Susan were feeling right now, but they must be strong for the sake of their children, she thought.

"Well, kids, the visit did not go the way we anticipated; life is unpredictable. In situations like this, no one can foresee how things will go; emotions are raw, everyone deals with grief in a different manner. This is a very tragic time in the life of this family. I hope that this will bring them closer together and that Lori and Susan will be open to our help. I will call tomorrow to see how Susan is doing."

"Mom, we still don't know if Lori is the girl from my school."

"In time, we will find that out, but in the meantime, we must pray for them," Mom responded.

Chapter 10

By the time they got back home, it was 6:30 p.m. Maria decided she would prepare a snack of crackers, cheese, and tea for everyone, and she would top it off with a slice of her mom's cake. She placed the snack in a tray and took it to Jamie and Karla, who were in the family room. "Thank you, Maria; we sure needed that."

"Mom, you must go to bed early tonight. We do not want you overdoing things; remember you were just in the hospital, and you will be going to work tomorrow. We will prepare breakfast and dinner as we promised, so you don't have to worry about anything," said Jamie.

"Thank you, Jamie. I am feeling a bit tired, so I'll go to bed as soon as I am finished here. Make sure both of you get to bed early tonight too. It has been quite an interesting weekend, and you have school in the morning."

Maria volunteered to wash the dishes since Jamie would be preparing breakfast the next morning. Jamie and Mom kissed Maria good night, and she went upstairs to bed. Maria hurriedly washed the dishes and went upstairs; she had to wait on the bathroom as Jamie was taking a shower, so she used the time to get her clothes ready for school. She had just finished and was about to sit when she heard the bathroom door opened, and Jamie's room door closing. He was finished in the bathroom, so she could take her shower. She had a lot to think about; she quickly showered and went to her bed. Her thoughts went back to Lori, and she felt a deep sense of sympathy for her. She reflected on how challenging life was for her after she had lost her father; she had felt so alone in her grief, yet she was not alone. Her mother and brother were experiencing the same loss and were grieving just as she was. She had often wondered if she could ever recover from the feeling of loss. *Death had a way of forcing us to grow up quicker than we would like to,* she thought. If it was so difficult for her to work through her grief, how much more difficult it was for Lori, who had witnessed the death of her sister. That image of her sister will always be in her memory. *I do hope Lori will allow me to help her and not shut me out. I know it is not easy, but she can get through this with the proper help.*

The alarm sounded, and Maria jumped out of bed. As she showered, she wondered if the Lori that was in her class at school was the same Lori who lost her sister. *Could it be coincidental that there were two Loris that share the same last name? I guess, in time, I will find out.* She hoped that she would have a good day without any form of bullying by her "persecutors." As she got dressed and combed her hair, she could hear Jamie in the kitchen preparing breakfast. He would be leaving for school soon, so she hurriedly finished dressing and went down to have breakfast with him.

"Had a good night, Pumpkin?"

"Yes, I did, although I spent the first hour thinking about Lori and her family."

"I think we all did; it brought back memories of our struggles to survive the pain and grief we felt after Dad died. I am confident they will come out of this with more love and with a stronger family bond, but it will take time. Speaking about time, it is time for me to get to school, so I will just run upstairs and tell Mom goodbye. You have a good day, and don't let those girls get to you."

"Thanks, Jamie, I will remember that."

After Jamie left for school, Maria brought a cup of tea upstairs to her mom and spent the rest of the time before going to catch the bus talking with her. Mom always had a soothing effect on her. "It's time for you to walk to the bus stop now, Maria. I love you, have a good day."

"Thanks, Mom, you too. Breakfast is on the table, and remember, do not worry about dinner; we will prepare it when we get home."

Maria was deep in thought as she walked to the bus stop. She reflected on the theme of the pastor's message on Sunday, not sure that she fully understood what he meant by "doing good to those who hate you and persecute you." She felt she was hated by her "persecutors" at school, and how would she handle it if any of them should decide to ridicule or bully her today? *Well, we will see if I am able to respond with kindness. Maybe that was the key to stopping the spate of bullying I had received over the last couple of months. It is worth a test, and I am going to give it my best shot.* When she thought of the tragedy in her own life and now the tragedy in Lori's family, she concluded that life was too short to be wasted on petty disagreements and differences. *If I could only get these girls to recognize that, then life would be good for us at school. I will try my hardest to set that example. Lord, I need Your strength and determination to win this battle.*

"Maria!"

She looked up to see John walking towards her and saying, "You are early, remember I promised to walk you to and from the bus stop until you felt comfortable walking by yourself. You seem fine, however. What brought about the change? You don't seem to be afraid anymore."

Maria brought John up to date on the events of the weekend. She explained to him why she was no longer afraid to walk alone to the bus stop. "But I am happy to see you because I still face the problem of bullying; I will try my best to respond positively to any negative situations that may arise. Although you are not in any of my classes, your being here to encourage me as I start my day makes me feel brave and more confident that I can do this. It would be nice if you could still ride the bus with me until I feel I can manage this on my own."

"I will meet you at the bus stop in the mornings."

"Thanks, John."

"You're welcome."

The bus pulled up, and the students began to get on. In the distance, Maria could see Terry running to catch the bus before it drove off. She was tempted to ignore Terry's shouts telling her to ask the driver to wait on her, but she remembered her resolve to love despite the treatment she had received from Terry in the past. She told Mr. James, the bus driver, that Terry was running to catch the bus and asked if he could wait on her. Mr. James glanced in his mirror and said, "Isn't that the girl who always gives you a tough time on the bus?"

"Yes, it is," Maria replied.

"Am I to understand that you are looking out for her after the treatment you have received at her hands?"

"Yes, I have made a resolution to treat her kindly, regardless of how she treats me. Maybe it will make a difference, and she will see that her behavior is wrong and stop. I am hoping that by setting an example of love instead of hate and by blessing those who treat me badly, bullies will reflect on their actions. Also, with the impact it has on others, they may purpose in their heart to stop hurting others. I don't know how this will play out, but I think it's worth a try, don't you?"

"Well, I guess that's one way to put it," Mr. James replied. "It would be wonderful if this turned out the way you hope, but I have lived longer than you, and I have seen too many bullies continue to hurt people right into adulthood. Some of them never learn, but then again, bullies are hurting, and they feel the need to hurt someone who they perceive to be weaker than they are."

"You see, they tend to have low self-esteem, and until we can help them to see that they are just as good as anyone else, and they begin to love themselves, and their self-esteem rises, they will not be able to feel good about themselves. They need to know that they don't have to be the product of their circumstances or their environment; they have the power to change how their life story ends."

Terry entered the bus panting from the run, "Thank you for holding the bus for me, Mr. James." She smiled at Maria as she walked past. John had listened to the entire conversation between Mr. James and Maria and shared with her how impressed he was at her boldness to try to live a life of integrity and righteousness. Maria thought she had begun to understand what her father had meant by "A soft answer turneth away wrath, but grievous words stir up anger." She knew what she had decided to do was not going to be easy: things would happen, she most likely would be hurt and ridiculed again, but she had to persevere with her plans. Would she really be able to withstand the temptation to react negatively?

Maria felt a bit nervous as the bus pulled into the bus loop. *Now the proof would be in the pudding, she thought. Will I be able to respond kindly to someone who treats me badly or talks negatively about me? If I find I cannot respond with kindness, then I will shut my mouth. It is better not to speak than to say something negative and cause a problem to escalate.* With this resolve, she stepped off the bus and hurried to class, determined to stick to her decisions while wishing she would not run into any of the girls in the clique.

On her way, her mind went back to the many times the girls had teased her about what she was wearing. They would point to her and laugh, "Ha, ha, ha, you got your clothes and shoes from Family Dollar or one of the dollar stores." She would pretend that what they said did not hurt her and respond sarcastically. One weekend, her mom had bought her a new outfit, and she was excited. She loved the pants and blouse and thought it complemented the color of her hair and brought out the color in her face. *I do not look so pale,* she thought. She strutted in front of the mirror, admiring herself, a feeling of confidence surging through her. So, that Monday morning, she was excited to put on her new outfit. She thought to herself no one would dare say anything negative about the way she was dressed. She knew she looked good in her outfit. Mom and Jamie had told her it was a perfect fit and that the colors suited her.

She stepped off the bus, head held high, glowing with confidence, but this feeling was short-lived when she heard Brianna and Angie laughing and looked around to see them pointing at her. "Look at those clothes," they shrieked with laughter, bringing students' attention to what she was wearing. She felt deflated, her confidence shattered, and her self-esteem sank to her feet; this was the last straw. Maria could feel anger bubbling inside; she got so angry that she swung her fist, hitting Angie square in the face. Angie hit the ground like a ton of bricks. Everyone was surprised; they had never seen Maria hit someone before, they began to laugh. Brianna stood there with her mouth wide open in disbelief. She was about to punch Brianna too when Lisa stepped in and held on to Maria's hand, stopping her from landing a punch in Brianna's face and telling her it was not worth it. Reality checked in when Angie said she would report her to the office. Maria knew she would be in trouble with administration and with her mom. *I will be suspended*, she thought. This was when Lisa and a few of the girls who had witnessed the interchange said they had seen the two girls bullying Maria many times, and they would tell the assistant principal that Maria was only defending herself. That was not exactly true, but Maria was not about to say anything to the contrary. She had gotten away with it that time, and she vowed she would never allow herself to get so angry again.

The interchange had caused their attacks on her to escalate, and every day during lunch, Angie, Brianna, Terry, and Lori sat together, and they would point at her as they laughed and talked. One good thing had come out of this altercation: Lisa became her friend, and she told her to ignore them. *I think they were afraid of Lisa,* she thought. How she missed her friend, she had moved away during the Christmas break and the bullying intensified. Maria began to feel the anger rising in her, but she reminded herself of her resolution to show kindness to her "enemies." She took a deep breath and continued to walk slowly towards the classroom.

"Maria, wait for me." She turned around to see Terry running to catch up with her. *This is strange,* Maria thought. *Terry talking to me, I never thought I would see that day. I wonder what she wants.* "Thank you for holding the bus for me this morning. I do appreciate it. I must also apologize for the way I have treated you in the past. You see, Lori and I were bullied too by Angie and Brianna, and to fit in, we joined the group. We knew that what we were doing was wrong, but we felt we had to protect ourselves from being the center of their jokes, and we allowed ourselves to be drawn into a hateful situation. We had to pretend that we were not interested in learning, and so our grades began to fall."

"My dad and mom gave me an ultimatum, and I have two weeks to bring my grades up. That is why on Friday, I tried to complete the math problem Mr. Jones placed on the board. Being able to work the problem correctly made me feel good. It reminded me of how well I used to do. Do you think Mr. Jones will change my seat? I would like to sit beside you if you don't mind, and I hope your friend Jackie will not feel that I have intruded on your friendship."

Looking bewildered as if it were a dream, Maria replied, saying, "Well, you can ask Mr. Jones. I think he will allow a seat change, especially if you pay attention and complete his assignments. I don't think Jackie will mind; she is a nice girl."

Maria was concerned about Angie's reaction to the turn of events and felt that her fury would come at Terry. "She is not going to be very happy," she related.

"I am prepared for the onslaught. I know her tactics and the way she thinks; however, it may be more vicious than I expect. I'll cross that bridge when I get there," Terry remarked.

"Alright. Jackie and I will stand up for you; I think they are not sure how Jackie will react if they were to try bullying us. But when Jackie is not there, they will try..."

Terry cut in, "It's still a bit early, so maybe we could go and see Mr. Jones and ask him to change my seat before the rest of the class comes in."

The girls rushed to the classroom and knocked on the door, but Mr. Jones was not inside. "We will just have to wait until he gets here or until class starts," Maria said.

Terry sighed, "It would be better to talk to him before the class; I am a bit nervous to ask him when the other students are coming in; I don't know how Angie will react. I guess I am still a bit intimidated by her, but all I know is we are done. I cannot allow myself to be pulled down any longer."

"Good morning, girls," Mr. Jones greeted.

"Good morning, Mr. Jones," they echoed in unison.

"You are early to class today."

"Yes, sir, can we talk to you?" Terry asked.

"Sure, come on in."

Terry explained the situation and asked if he could move her to the empty seat beside Maria or to the front of the classroom. She explained that she did not want to be seated near Angie because of the distraction, plus she wanted to concentrate on her schoolwork. Mr. Jones was happy about Terry's decision to focus and agreed to the move. He put her at the front of the class beside Jackson. Jackson was an exceptional student in all his classes except math; he had quite a challenge understanding some math concepts, although he tried very hard.

"Terry," Mr. Jones remarked. "I know you have the ability to excel in math, so I am giving you the responsibility of assisting Jackson during class. I want you to lead the extra team we formed recently during the breakout sessions. Helping others will reinforce your own learning. You have made a very important decision, young lady, and I am happy to see that you will no longer join in destructive behavior against other students. I am proud of you."

Terry knew he was talking about the way she and Angie had treated Maria and some other members of the class, and she vowed that she would never again get involved in negative behaviors, especially bullying.

The bell sounded, and the other students began to file into the classroom. Maria was curious to see Angie's reaction when she saw Terry seated at the front of the class. *I wonder how Terry is going to deal with Angie's onslaught and sarcasm; this is going to be very interesting.* She hoped that embracing Terry would not affect her relationship with Jackie. She wished Jackie would come in before the late bell, so she could bring her up to date about the discussions she had with Terry.

Her thoughts were interrupted by Jackie saying, "Hi, Maria, how was your weekend?"

"Good, but I need to talk to you about something. Did you notice that Terry's seat has changed?"

"Oh, as a matter of fact, I did not. What caused the change?"

Maria explained to Jackie and suggested that they encourage Terry in her decisions. "She would not have to do this alone; we would stand up for her as you stood up for me. Thank you, I consider you a very good friend, and I admire the way you do not let anyone get under your skin; you stand up for what you believe in. I think together we can make a difference and maybe change the way things happen in our classrooms."

"How can I say no when you put it like that? To be honest, when you started talking, I felt as if Terry would be intruding on our friendship, but I can now see how this would benefit all of us. I only caution you to let us take this slowly; she has been friends with Angie for nearly one year. What makes you think there will be a drastic change in her behavior?"

"Well, let's give her the benefit of the doubt."

"Okay, I agree with you, we can all be friends, but we have to let our guard down slowly."

"Maria, Jackie, are you working on the problem on the whiteboard, or are you just talking?" Mr. Jones asked.

"Getting to it, sir," Maria responded.

The late bell went, and Mr. Jones called Terry to the board. Terry was a bit nervous, but she knew she had worked the problem correctly in her notebook. She solved the problem and explained each step. Mr. Jones was impressed by her; you could see his pleasure in the way he beamed.

"Great job, Terry," he said.

As Terry walked back to her seat, the door opened, and Angie came in; she gave Mr. Jones a late pass and went to her seat. She was surprised when Terry sat in front and did not sit in her usual seat beside her. She beckoned to Terry to come sit beside her, but Terry ignored her. It seemed the whole class held their breath in anticipation, waiting for Angie to say something negative, but she just sat there in stunned disbelief.

"The class is unusually quiet today," Jackson remarked to Terry, who was sitting beside him.

"Yes, it is. Did you understand the problem that I solved on the board?"

"I think I got it."

"If you ever have difficulty with any of the math concepts, let me know, and I will explain them to you."

"Thank you, but I thought you were not good at math. You solved and explained the problem beautifully."

"Well, you see, I am good at math, and I really like it; I just pretended not to like it because of the company I was keeping. But things have changed, I must pull my grades up, or I will be in trouble with my parents. We have most of our classes together, and I have a problem with my graphic design class, so can you help me? I am not very creative."

"Sure, we can help each other."

"That's a deal."

All too soon, the bell rang, and everyone quickly packed up their books and headed out the door. No one wanted to be late to class. The principal, Mrs. Hibbert, had announced that all teachers should lock their door when the late bell rang, and if anyone was seen outside a classroom after the bell, the hall monitors would take their names, and they would be given a detention and a call home. The teachers had complained that too many students were turning up for their classes late with no valid excuses. Terry quickly made her way towards Jackie and Maria.

"Hi, Terry," Jackie said. "Welcome to our group. I want you to understand if you join our group, you must be prepared to focus on all your classes and bring up your grades. We will set an example in conduct and academics, and we will be respectful to everyone. Is that understood?"

"I agree to the conditions of our friendship."

"So, no more bullying, and I expect you to treat Angie with respect, regardless of what she says and how she behaves," she concluded.

Maria respected Jackie for her forthrightness; she might appear tough on the outside, but Maria knew she was soft on the inside. Terry would soon get to understand Jackie. *I hope Terry was not offended and realized that Jackie only meant well,* she thought. As they hurried to class, Jackie remarked. "I have not seen Lori in school for close to a week. What's up with her, Terry?"

"Oh, there is a tragedy in her family. Her little sister Joanna was hit by a car and died. I hear Lori is taking it very hard."

"That is so sad. I can't imagine how she must be feeling."

"Are you in touch with her?"

"No, we heard about it from someone in her neighborhood who knows the family. We don't keep in touch outside of school."

"Oh, that is so sad; I understand her grief. I lost my mother recently, and Maria lost her father also. We know how devastating that can be. Our thoughts and prayers are with her."

Maria's suspicions that the family she had visited was Lori's family were confirmed, but she did not think it was the right moment to say anything. She would keep this to herself until the appropriate time.

"Maria, you are unusually quiet," Jackie remarked.

"I am just thinking how hard this is for Lori to lose a sister. One never expects to lose a loved one, especially one so young. It teaches us that we are to treasure every moment with our family and friends; no one knows when tragedy will strike."

The girls split up for classes. Terry was going to her class and Jackie and Maria were going to their language arts class. While Terry made her way to her social studies class, she ran into Angie, who seemed to have been waiting for her. Angie demanded to know two things: why had Terry walked to class with Jackie and Maria and not waited for her, and why was she sitting at the front of the math class. Terry felt her armpits getting wet with sweat. She would have been naive to think that Angie would let this slide and not confront her. She realized she was not quite ready to handle the onslaught of words and the drama that Angie was famous for. Many people had experienced her tongue lashing, and Terry felt fearful.

However, she was determined that she would not allow Angie to intimidate her any longer, and she took a deep breath before responding. "I am tired of being your puppet and catering to all your demands, it is not okay to bully people, and I will no longer pretend to be dumb to make you feel good about yourself."

"Are you saying I am dumb?"

"You said it, not me, so you decide. You have been a major distraction in my life, but no more. I have decided to pay attention in my classes and complete all my assignments. I have two weeks to bring my grades up."

Angie opened her mouth, but no words came out; she appeared to be stunned. The dreaded Angie was at a loss for words. Terry felt sorry for her but was a bit amused to see the expression on Angie's face, as she looked like a fish gasping for water; her eyes widened with disbelief.

"I am sorry that I ever joined you in bullying anyone. This is not me; I have to be true to myself and be who I was meant to be, that means my behavior must reflect my convictions."

Angie finally regained her composure. "Who do you think you are? As if I really cared about you. You are so lame. I befriended you because no one else wanted to be your friend, and this is the way you repay me?"

"Angie, you are selfish, and when you start thinking of others and less of yourself, maybe you will find a true friend. It is always all about you and what you want, and your behavior is destructive. It is time that I do what is right. I am no longer afraid of you, Angie. Maybe if you took the time to consider others, life would be better for everyone."

The bell sounded, and Terry rushed to her class, knowing she would get a detention and a call home for being late. *But if I explain to Mom and Dad why I was late, I am sure they will understand that I had to deal with this situation and face my fears.* Whatever the consequences, Terry felt good within herself, she had stood up to the school's biggest bully, and she was no longer afraid.

The rest of the day went well—no drama. Maria noticed that when she passed Angie in the hallway, she was unusually quiet. It was hard to think that Angie was in school, and no one heard her loud voice shouting at or making fun of another student. Maria began to feel sorry for her. She recalled what Mr. James, the bus driver, had said to her, "A bully is usually someone who has been bullied or is being bullied at home, and they become so angry that they take out their frustrations on others by bullying them." *I wonder if this is the case with Angie, Maria thought. I think I will try to reach out to her and get to know her a little better. She must feel as if she is losing all her friends because Terry has pulled away from her and Lori has not been in school. She only has Brianna left for now. I hope Lori chooses to do what is right when she gets back. I will certainly try to help her through her tragedy and be there for her.*

It was the end of the day, and Maria walked to the bus engrossed in her thoughts. As she boarded the bus, she spotted John hurrying towards the bus loop and kept a seat beside her for him.

"Thanks for saving me a seat."

"You know I'll always save you a seat."

Terry came in, bent down beside her, and told her that she had a conversation with Angie and told her that she could no longer hang out with her.

"Good for you," Maria replied as Terry made her way to her seat near the back of the bus.

"Isn't that one of the girls who usually bully you?" John remarked.

"Usually is the operative word," Maria replied. "But not again." Maria proceeded to bring John up to date on the day's events.

"Remarkable," John exclaimed. "Well, I would never have guessed this would happen so quickly. Keep doing what you have been doing; it seems to have brought about positive results."

Chapter 11

The bus came to a stop, and John and Maria got off.

"John, thank you for riding the bus with me these last few days, but I am no longer afraid, and I will no longer be bullied on the bus, as you can see. I will call to thank your mom for allowing you to take the bus to and from school and walk me home. See you tomorrow."

They parted ways, each heading in the opposite direction. Maria waved to Terry, who was seated at the back of the bus. She wondered what was going through the minds of the other students who had watched the interchange between the two girls. *But then, that is their business. I am only happy that Terry has decided to do what was right for her.* She walked home thinking of how surprised her mom and Jamie would be when they learned that the Lori who lost her little sister Joanna was the Lori from her school.

Maria opened the door and was greeted by the smell of the meal Jamie was cooking, and it made her realize how hungry she was. She felt a little guilty that she was not helping as much as she had planned and was determined to take charge of cleaning up after dinner. As she made her way to the kitchen, she called out to Jamie to let him know she was home.

"What are you cooking?"

"Oh, I thought I would make some lamb chops with sweet potato, beans, and carrots. It should be ready in about fifteen to twenty minutes."

"It's one of Mom's favorite dishes, and it smells delicious. I am so hungry; I cannot wait for dinner to be ready. I feel I am not keeping my end of the bargain because you are doing most of the cooking. Therefore, I will clean up after dinner; that should give you time to study and do your homework."

"That's okay, Pumpkin, I am home earlier than you, so it's only fair that I take charge of the cooking, and yes, it would be great if you do the dishes after dinner."

"Something happened at school today, which I will share with you when Mom gets home. I'll just run upstairs and take a shower before dinner."

"Maria, dinner is ready, and I'm hungry. Hurry up so we can eat together."

"I'll be down in a jiffy, Jamie. I'm almost done."

Jamie could hear his stomach protesting. He was happy that he had cooked enough so everyone could have a second serving. The family loved lamb chops and potatoes, and he felt that he had done a very good job.

It had paid off to watch Mom and Dad when they were cooking. During those times, he and Maria would sit in the kitchen and talk about challenges or share little anecdotes from school. Dad would pipe in with stories of his day in the flower shop. Jamie missed those times. The ringing of the telephone brought him back to reality. It was Officer Jones who was in the neighborhood and wanted to stop by to talk to Karla about their visit to the Thomas family.

"I'm sorry, Officer Jones, but Mom is not in right now and won't be home for another hour. Wait a minute; I hear the front door opening." Jamie had hardly finished his words when his mom walked in. She looked a little tired but happy. She could smell the delicious aroma of the food Jamie had cooked. "Mom," Jamie called. "Officer Jones is in the neighborhood and wants to know if he could come by. He wants an update on the visit we had yesterday with the Thomas family. Are you up for a visit, Mom?"

"I'm a bit tired, but it is okay since you kids made sure that I have nothing to do when I get home but put my feet up. Maybe he could join us for dinner."

"Sure, Mom, I'll let him know, but there goes my second serving," Jamie muttered under his breath. Officer Jones accepted the invitation and told them he would be there in five minutes. "I'm sure Maria will be down by then," Jamie remarked.

The doorbell rang, and Maria, who had just come downstairs, shouted that she would answer the door. "We're expecting Officer Jones, and he'll be staying for dinner." Really, Maria's mind went on overdrive; she was still matchmaking in her mind. Officer Jones really liked her mom, and Mom was more tolerant of him. *Maybe something will work out between them, but I dare not suggest such a thing. Mom would be very upset.* She opened the door and invited the policeman in; he looked a bit hungry, and Maria knew that he was in for a treat. *Wait until he tastes a slice of Mom's cake,* she thought. *He will be hooked on her for life.*

"Come and join us at the table, Officer Jones. Dinner is served."

"Thank you, ma'am," he replied. "It sure smells good."

Officer Jones and Maria joined Jamie and Karla at the table, and Mrs. Rodriquez said, "Jamie, will you say the grace before dinner."

"Yes, Mom." Jamie was hungry, so his prayer was short; he could not wait to dig in.

"How did the visit to the Thomases go?" the cop inquired.

Karla filled Officer Jones in on the visit and told him that they did not meet the daughter Lori who had taken the death of her sister very hard, to which Maria disclosed that Lori was the girl from her school whose little sister Joanna died. She went on to fill them in on the details of what had taken place at school that day.

"I'm so proud of you, Maria," Mom remarked.

"You did well, little sis," chimed in Jamie.

"I really would like to help Lori if she will let me, given our history and everything."

The conversation was interrupted by the ringing of the telephone, and Karla got up to answer. "Hello, oh, hi Jack, how is your family doing?"

"Not so well, I am afraid; I really need your help. Could you come over this evening? I know it is late and everything, but I do not know how to help my family through this time. The funeral is tomorrow afternoon, and I do not know how we are going to get through this. I feel powerless right now. I don't even know how I will survive tomorrow, and I am no help to them. There is not much conversation in our home; nobody talks about the death, as if silence can turn back the hands of time."

Karla listened, not saying much. *What can one say in a time like this?* she thought. *He just needs someone to listen to him.* "Sometimes words are inadequate in describing our feelings. We are having dinner; as soon as we are finished, we'll be over. Officer Jones is here; I will ask him if he would be able to come over too if that is okay with you."

"That's alright."

"You see, he has had tragedy in his life as well, so talking to a man who has walked in your shoes will help you. Let me find out if he is available to come." Officer Jones agreed.

"It's settled then, Jack. We will all be there in about two hours."

"Thank you. I'll talk to my family about you coming over."

She hung the phone. "He did this back way," Mom commented. "He should have discussed this with his family before calling us; they may not want anyone over the day before the funeral. But we have promised, so we will go. Let us pray about this visit that the Lord will give us wisdom and guide us in our speech so we know when to speak, what to say, and when to listen. Also, that each member of the family would be willing and ready to talk about their feelings and accept the help that is offered."

"Let us finish eating so we can get over there quickly. We do not want to stay too late," Jamie urged.

They hurriedly finished eating; Maria cleared the table and washed the dishes while Jamie went to take a shower. Karla offered Officer Jones a slice of her famous cake.

"Thank you; I never refuse a slice of cake." Karla handed him the slice of cake. "Thank you; I certainly will enjoy it. Oh, this is very delicious."

"Thank you; it's one of my children's favorite."

"I can see why."

Officer Jones fidgeted for a while as if he was nervous, then he said, "May I call you Karla?"

"Sure."

"And I would like you to call me Mark if you don't mind."

The conversation was interrupted by Maria and Jamie joining them in the family room. "We are ready if you both are," remarked Jamie.

"We can all go in my car," Mark suggested.

"That would be swell; we'll get there quicker, and I won't get hot walking," Maria chirped.

Karla called Jack to let him know they would be there in five minutes. "That's great, thank you," Jack replied.

Lori again had elected to stay in her room. Jack said she did not feel like talking. The rest of the family had joined them downstairs; neither Susan nor Chris were talking. The silence was deafening. *I can almost hear myself think,* Maria thought to herself. There was an uncomfortable feeling of being in a place where you were not wanted. The silence was suddenly broken by Jack. As Karla listened to him speak, she could not help but sense that Jack was very angry with himself, but why? There was nothing he could have done to change the situation, or was there more to the story than he had shared? Jack slumped his shoulders as if in despair. His next words made her feel that he was filled with regret, but regret for what? Why? It was almost as if he blamed himself for his daughter's death; how could that be when he was not even there? "Maybe it would help if you just spoke about how you feel and how the loss is affecting you. I sense you are blaming yourself, Jack, and there was nothing you could have done," Karla said as she encouraged him to share his feelings.

Jack cleared his throat and shifted in his chair as if he were uncomfortable. Then he spoke softly, "I was supposed to take Joanna to school that morning, but as usual, I was rushing to work and told Lori to walk her to the bus stop. You see, I spend a lot of time at work, meeting deadlines and trying to prove myself with the hope of moving up the corporate ladder. Susan begged me many times to slow down; she said I did not need to prove myself to her, that the children needed me, and I should try to spend more time with the family."

"You see, I grew up in a loving family, but we were poor and could not afford the nice clothes and shoes that other children could. I decided to work hard in school, pay attention in class, complete my assignments, and keep my grades up. I wanted to be successful in life, so I vowed that when I had my own family, my children would never experience what I went through, they would not lack anything, and I would see to it that all their needs and wants were met. I provided for them financially; they had all that they wanted, but they did not have my time. I was too busy making money. I gave up the opportunity of having a happy, loving family for riches, but look at what it cost me. It cost me the life of my daughter."

"I cannot even remember the last time I told anyone in my family that I loved them. Had I taken the time to take Joanna to school that morning, she would still be alive," he sobbed. "I am to blame for Joanna's death. I tried to put the total blame on the driver of the car but had I taken her to school that morning, she would not have lost her life. I do not have much of a relationship with my children because I was hardly there for them, and now it is too late for me to change that for Joanna. In trying to prove myself a success to the world, I have lost what matters most, my wife and my children."

"Jack, we all make mistakes, and it is not too late for change. Your family is here now, and you can ask them to forgive you. You have the chance to make things right and start over. Jack, it is never too late," Karla repeated gently.

"How can they ever forgive me?"

"Daddy, I forgive you," Lori whispered. She had come down the stairs without anyone noticing and was standing some distance behind Jack's chair. Jack jumped out of his seat, ran to Lori, and hugged her and told her he loved her. "Thank you; I don't deserve it. I promise things will be different from now on. Lori, don't ever blame yourself again. This was not your fault; you could not have prevented the accident."

He went over to Susan and hugged her, "Can you forgive me, Susan?"

Susan shook her head and said, "I have forgiven you, Jack, but it will take some time for me to heal."

"Thank you for loving me and putting up with my selfishness. I am sorry for neglecting you and the kids; you have been a wonderful, faithful wife and mother to our children, and I will try to make it up to you. Chris, I promise to spend more time with you. Because I spent more time at work than I did at home with my family, you have had to take on more responsibility than you should. I love you, son. Please, forgive me."

"Losing Joanna has reminded me that life is short, and we should endeavor to spend as much time as we can with those we love. Money does not make anyone happy, but love, laughter, and time spent with your family do. These are things that cannot be bought; they are more important than wealth. It will not be easy for any of us tomorrow, but together we will get through this. Chris, do not ever make the same mistakes I made. When you have your own family, always be there for them. Will you promise me, son?"

"I will, Dad, I promise."

Mark had not spoken through the entire time the family was visiting. He looked at Karla with admiration, thinking to himself what a remarkable woman she was. She had encouraged Jack to talk about his feelings and, in doing so, the family seemed to be headed towards healing. He hoped that out of this tragedy would come a blessing. He felt a stirring within him; for the first time since he had lost his wife, he was taking note of another woman. He really liked Karla and was thinking to himself, *Maybe, in time, I will ask her out on a date. I hope she does not turn me down.*

His thoughts were interrupted by Karla telling Jack and Susan that it was time to go. They would leave so the family could have some privacy. "What time is the funeral tomorrow?"

"It will be at four in the afternoon."

"If you don't mind, we would like to attend the funeral in support of your family."

"That would be nice, Karla," Susan replied.

"Please do come; I would really appreciate it, and thank you for your kindness."

Maria got up, went over to Lori, and hugged her. "It will be okay, Lori; it took me some time to get past my father's sudden death too. If you need to talk, I am here for you."

Lori gave a half-smile.

"Don't worry about anything at school; things will get better," she added. Lori understood what Maria was saying, and she was grateful for that assurance.

"Thank you," she replied.

"I'll see you tomorrow."

Mark opened the door for Karla to get in the car. As he shut the door, he glanced at her, thinking how beautiful she was. *I must not get ahead of myself here,* he thought. *I am sure Karla would never be interested in me.*

"Thank you, Mark, for taking us to visit the Thomases. I do hope they will keep moving towards healing and love."

"You're welcome. I am glad for the privilege of taking you and your family, and I am grateful for that dinner and dessert. Both were very delicious."

"You're welcome. I see we are home now. Thanks again for the ride."

"If you would like, I could take you to the funeral tomorrow; it's my day off."

"Thank you, Mark, that is nice of you; we'd surely appreciate that."

Mark watched as Karla came out of the car and headed towards the house. She turned and waved at him before closing the door behind her.

"It is time for bed, kids. Jamie, you will be home by two, and tomorrow is an early release day for you, Maria, so both of you will be home in time to attend the funeral. I will request the afternoon off. I am sure they will approve it because apart from when I was sick, I have never taken a day or requested time off."

"Good night, Mom," the kids echoed in unison.

"Good night, my dears," Mom responded.

Maria lay in her bed, reflecting on the events of the day. Things have a way of changing suddenly when you least expect it. Terry had made a bold decision to pull out of the clique, and she followed it up by telling Angie how she felt. Lori and her family had made a step in the right direction by facing their problems head-on. *It all started with forgiveness,* she thought, *and they sure expressed that.* It would not be easy, but it would be worth it in the end. Then, there was Mark. Maria had seen the way he looked at her mother, but she did not dare suggest this to Mom. They would make a good team, Maria thought. She secretly hoped that in time Mark would show his interest to Mom, and she would reciprocate the feelings. Before long, she was fast asleep.

Chapter 12

Mark drove off slowly. He had not thought about another woman since the death of his wife. Oh, how he had loved Jane; she was beautiful, uncomplicated, and full of fun. She had a vibrant personality, which lit up every room she entered, and she had a way of bringing out the best in others. When she had told him she was expecting their first child, he thought that life was perfect. He was the happiest man he knew. But that joy did not last because his beloved Jane and their baby had died. He thought about the death of his wife and child and how angry he was at God. He had blamed Him for taking his family, and for months, he could not seem to shake the feeling of grief and loss. For a while, he had lost interest in life; he thought he could not go on without her and how unfair this was that he had lost both his wife and child. Whenever he saw a husband and wife with a child, he remembered his own family, which was no more.

Loneliness had set in because he had isolated himself from friends and family. He needed to grieve, and no one could help him with that; it was something he had to do on his own, or so he had thought, until Officer Hugh Mackenzie, a new officer to the unit, befriended him.

Hugh was easy to talk to, and Mark felt the wall he had built around his heart begin to fall away. He found himself sharing with Hugh things he had not dared to tell anyone else. It felt good having someone to talk with about the emotional struggle that followed the death of his family. He told him about his feelings of blame, wanting to die, and hopelessness. Although he was not to blame for Jane and his son's death, he wondered if she would still be alive if he had not suggested that they have a baby. Hugh, who had studied psychology and counseling before joining the police force, used his knowledge and experience to help him through the grieving process until he began to heal. It was an emotional roller coaster, but eventually, the emotional rides became less tumultuous until he got to the point where he could laugh again. Now, was he ready to love again?

He turned in his driveway, parked in the garage, and hopped out of the car with a spring in his step. He had not felt this way in a long time; he had missed the feeling of caring for someone other than himself. He could feel his emotions stirring within him whenever he thought of Karla or was in her company. "I am attracted to her," he said to himself. "But she does not seem to be interested in me in any way. I am fooling myself. Pull yourself together, Mark Jones," he said, startling himself—he had not realized he had spoken aloud. He began to think about his life, his childhood through high school, the challenges he had faced growing up, and the person who influenced and encouraged him to attend the police academy.

Mark entered the house still thinking about his younger years. *I have certainly come a long way,* he thought. *Growing up, I never thought about the challenges or pain any adult could experience. I only knew that I wanted to grow up quickly, so I could make my own decisions, go where I wanted to go, and do what I wanted to do.*

Mark was born in Brooklyn, New York. It was a rough neighborhood, and his mother had kept him in the house as much as possible. She would walk him to school and pick him up on her lunch break with the hope of keeping him safe, away from the drugs and violence in his neighborhood. There was no one else to help her as his dad had left home years ago when he was three, and his younger brother was only one. He would go home to an empty house as his mom could not afford to send him to aftercare because she had to pay for his brother in daycare.

The other boys had teased him, calling him momma's boy, "Your momma has to walk you home from school every day." His mom thought if she walked him to and from school, she would be able to protect him from the negative influences in the neighborhood. His mother's intentions were good, but they caused him a lot of pain as the boys continuously teased him at school. It was hard for him to walk in the neighborhood without someone passing derogatory remarks about him.

Most of the boys in his neighborhood were involved in either gangs or drugs; they would break into cars, homes, and even hold up stores and people on the street. His mother wanted better for him and his brother, so she made every effort to keep them away from the negative influences in his neighborhood. His brother started to hang out with some guys in the neighborhood, and he got in with the wrong crowd and ended up joining one of the gangs. This broke his mother's heart; the thing she dreaded most was now a part of her life. Her family had become one of the statistics in the neighborhood. Her only solace was the fact that Mark had not become a part of any of the gangs. Mark had several conversations with his brother Tom with the hope that his brother would get out of the gang.

Tom informed his brother Mark that if he were to get out of the gang, he would have to move out of the neighborhood and maybe go to another state. Mark discussed this with his mother, and they decided to move to Florida. "That should be far enough," his mother had said. If that was what it would take to save her son, she was going to do it. The leader of the gang, who they called Big Ed, got "wind" that Tom was leaving, and the night before they were scheduled to move to Florida, Tom was gunned down by a member of his own gang. It was a miracle that Tom regained consciousness and survived his injuries, but he had a praying mother who believed that her son would not die.

Mark purposed in his heart that as soon as his brother was well and out of hospital, they would move to Florida as planned. The move to Florida was a good one. Tom turned his life around, completed high school, and went to college. He became a successful lawyer in St. Petersburg and insisted that their mother move to St. Petersburg and live with him. By then, Mark had become a police officer and was at the time dating Jane, who he married soon after. Mark decided he would stay in West Palm Beach. After Jane and his son died, his mother and brother visited him and stayed for the funeral. Tom went back to St. Petersburg while his mother stayed for one month to help him through the grieving process. *Those were tough days,* Mark said to himself. *Things are looking up, and I feel alive again.*

Chapter 13

The morning came too quickly. Maria jumped out of bed excited about the turn of events and all that had transpired within the last forty-eight hours. As she got dressed, she reflected on the challenges she had faced in school. *It did not mean that the bullying was over because Angie would not give up that easily, but life has a way of surprising us, she thought. Who would ever think that the clique would begin to dismantle? I feel that Lori will also pull away, and I do not think she would want to continue with her destructive behavior. Tragedy has a way of helping us appreciate our loved ones more.* Maria believed as Lori's family healed, her behavior would change, and she would focus on things that were important to her future and her life. *Maybe we could be friends, and she could become a part of our group. I had better get cracking and get dressed, or I will be late for school.*

Maria quickly showered and got dressed. As she combed her hair, she could hear movement in the kitchen and knew either her mom or Jamie was preparing breakfast. She still had time because her school started later than Jamie's. If she were not downstairs when he was leaving, he would shout to her that he was leaving for school, but Maria liked to spend time with her brother before he left for school. She always made the effort to be dressed and downstairs before he was ready to leave. Jamie had the ability to brighten her day with a compliment, a smile, a wise word, or just reminding her of who she was. He liked to say, "Pumpkin, remember you are a daughter of the King, so hold your head up and walk as if you are royalty because you are, you belong to the Most High God. You are His handiwork, and He makes no mistakes, so be happy. Love you." He would then give her a kiss on the cheek and run out the door. She really needed his reassurance this morning because she knew Angie would not be happy with the turn of events, and she needed strength and courage to face the challenges she envisioned would be waiting for her at school.

"Jamie, Maria," her mom called from the dining room. "Breakfast is ready." She quickly glanced at the clock and hurried to pin up her hair. If she got downstairs quickly, it would give her about twenty minutes with Jamie before he left for school, then she could spend some time with her mom before they left for work and school. She stopped to pick out the dress she would be wearing to Lori's sister Joanna's funeral.

There would not be a lot of time between getting home and getting to the funeral. She could hear her mother calling her again. Jamie was already downstairs having breakfast; she could hear them talking. Maria hurried down to join them; breakfast was always a pleasant experience for the family because since their dad died, that was the only meal they could sometimes sit and eat together.

As she sat down, Mom enquired of Maria how she felt about going to school and seeing Angie and Brianna. Maria responded, "Mom, I will remember who I am and whose I am, I am a daughter of the Most High King, and I will try my best not to let Him down. I will also remember the words that Dad always spoke to me, 'A soft answer turneth away wrath, but grievous words stir up anger.'"

"It seems as if you now understand that verse of Scripture, Maria," Jamie quirked.

"It is a verse of Scripture! I had no idea; no wonder it sounded so un-English if there is such a word. I am not there yet, but I think I am beginning to understand."

"You are growing up, Pumpkin; Dad would be so proud of you. I've got to run, see you later, Pumpkin, and remember whose daughter you are and act accordingly. Love you, Mom," Jamie shouted as he blew her a kiss and headed for the door.

"Don't forget we are going to the funeral later, so be home on time," Mom responded.

With Jamie gone off to school, it gave Maria a little time alone with her mom. Karla's job had adjusted her work time to nine to five; therefore, she left for work the same time Maria would leave for school. This meant that she would be home by six, get an hour's rest, eat, and head off to her second job, where she cleaned a lawyer's office from eight to ten. The money she received for those extra ten hours of work each week went towards grocery. "You know, Maria, we are blessed because we can pay all our bills, and we have never gone to our beds hungry, tired maybe, but not hungry. That is a lot to be thankful for. There are other young people just like you who go to bed hungry many nights because there is nothing to eat, so never take your blessings for granted. Promise me that you will always have a heart for those who are in need and extend help whenever you can."

"It is not your responsibility or your business to determine if they are genuine or not; just let your heart speak to you and respond to the gentle nudging of your heart. I am proud of you; you have been making some wise decisions lately, and you have not allowed your emotions to cloud your good judgment."

"Thanks, Mom, it has been an uphill struggle, and I have not yet mastered my emotions, but I am getting there. Thanks to you and Jamie for your daily support and encouragement."

Karla glanced at the clock on the wall, "Oh, how time flies, it's time for us to go catch our buses, or we will be late."

In a matter of minutes, both were headed out the door going in opposite directions to catch their bus. Maria turned and glanced at her mother as she walked briskly towards the bus stop. She was grateful her mother was alive and well. She thought about how close they had come to losing her and recognized the importance of celebrating each day as a gift. "One never knows what the next minute or day holds," she whispered to herself. Maria realized that she had taken up the habit of speaking her thoughts out loud and hoped she would not do this when anyone else was around. *They may think I am crazy,* she thought as she muffled a laugh. She could see the bus approaching in the distance, so she picked up her steps, not wanting to miss the bus.

Maria greeted Terry as she approached the stop. She could see from the faces of some of the students waiting to board the bus that they were a bit confused. Others looked on indifferently; they were in their own world, either listening to music, talking on their phones, or texting. Nothing seemed to interest or excite them. Others just stood around with a blank look on their faces, as if life were boring and they were going to school only because they had to. She thought of her own life and how colorful it was. She had a family who loved and cared for her, and there was never a dull moment in her house because the family found joy in the little things of life. *Life happens,* she thought to herself, *and the way we handle the challenges we face will determine how quickly recovery from negative situations would take.* Her heart was sad for the students who did not have the family support that she had; how hard it must be for them.

"Maria, get on the bus," Terry called out to Maria, who was so lost in her thoughts that she had not realized that everyone else had boarded the bus. She hopped on and sat beside Terry. "You looked as if you were far away in thoughts. Penny for them," Terry laughed.

"I was just thinking how blessed I am to have a loving family and good friends. Some of the students on the bus do not seem to have that, as they appear to be so indifferent and, for want of a better word, cold. Just existing, not living. But let me think about better things." They laughed and chatted the entire way to school.

"Well, we are here. This should be an interesting day, Maria; let us make the best of it."

They got off the bus and linked up with Jackie as she came off her bus. They talked all the way to math class. Mr. Jones had already placed the problem of the day on the whiteboard, so they sat down quietly and began to work the problem. Maria completed the assignment on the board before the bell rang and settled into her favorite pastime: daydreaming. She could not believe the turn of events. At last, she felt accepted: she had two friends in math class, the bullying had subsided quite a bit, and she no longer felt as angry as before. She had reached out to others who were in need and had reaped the benefits. *Anger really does not help,* she thought. *Only love does.* She wondered if Lori would join the group so they all could help her through the healing process.

Her thoughts were interrupted when a hand placed a note on her desk. She looked up to see Brianna moving away. She glanced back at Maria as she sat in her chair. Maria unfolded the note, not knowing what to expect. As she read it, she could feel the anger building up inside her. *I do not believe that girl,* she thought to herself. *I must remember the promise I made to myself to respond with kindness, but I am so angry right now.* Maria passed the note to Jackie, who exclaimed, "I don't believe this."

"I don't believe what?" Mr. Jones asked.

"It's not very important, sir. I'm sorry for the outburst."

"Make sure this does not happen in my class again. Have you finished solving the problem?"

"Yes, sir."

"Well, get to the board and work it for the class to see." That was a reminder that they needed to focus on Mr. Jones' class.

Maria became a bit sidetracked as her thoughts went back to the note Brianna had placed on her desk. The nerve of her to even think she would engage in a fight with her was unexpected. This was a threat, and maybe she should show the note to Mr. Jones. It appeared that Angie had used Brianna to challenge her to a fight and indicated that she would be waiting for her after school in the bus loop. The note also stated that Maria had turned Terry against her and had sabotaged their friendship. She decided that she would meet with Mr. Jones after the class and show him the note. She was not going to engage in a fight, and she was trying her best to be calm.

A few minutes before the class ended, Maria asked Mr. Jones if she could speak with him after class. She told Terry she should go ahead to class; she had to meet with Mr. Jones. She then handed Mr. Jones the note and told him it came from Brianna. He read the note and stopped Brianna as she headed out the door. "Young lady, I would like a word with you. Did you write this note?"

"No, sir, I did not."

"Did you pass this note to Maria?"

"Yes, sir."

"Did you know what was in the note?"

"No, sir."

"Who gave you the note?"

"Terry, sir."

"When did she give you the note?"

"This morning before school."

"I don't understand. Terry came in with Maria this morning, and I watched them take their seats and begin working on the assignment. You, on the other hand, came in sometime later, and you had no interchange with Terry. When could Terry have given you the note?"

"She gave it to me before class. I saw her in the courtyard, and she stopped to talk to me. She told me that Maria was harassing her, and she was going to put a stop to it once and for all. So, she asked me to pass the note to her, and I agreed to do it for her because she is my friend."

"And you did not care about her enough to stop her from doing something so stupid."

"That is not true, sir. Terry rode the bus with me, and we were together until we got in the classroom," Maria remarked.

"I will go with you both to the principal's office. Does any of you know what class Terry has now?"

"Yes, sir," Maria replied. "She has language arts class with Miss Lewis. I have the same class as her."

"Okay, I will have the office call through to Miss Lewis' classroom and have Terry meet us there. I'll walk you both down to the office."

Terry was already in the office when they got there. Mrs. Hibbert offered them a seat and began questioning Brianna. Brianna changed her story twice, and Mr.

Jones indicated that he was told a different story. Terry and Maria were able to explain that they rode the same bus, sat together, and went to class together, so Brianna had no opportunity to converse with Terry before class. There was also no opportunity for a note to be passed between them. Maria took the opportunity to share with the principal and Mr. Jones the struggles she had faced in the past with Brianna and Angie. Terry informed them that this only came about because she decided to get out of the clique and focus on her schoolwork. Mrs. Hibbert said she would deal with Angie; she gave Brianna a stern warning and sent them back to class.

Maria could not have asked for a better outcome. Brianna appeared as if she was losing steam; she no longer seemed to have that negative energy to fight. *Maybe she will leave us alone.* The rest of the day went smoothly; being an early release day, classes ended at 12:30 p.m., which gave Maria enough time to get home and get dressed for the funeral.

Chapter 14

When Maria got home from school, both Jamie and her mom were already there; she could hear the showers going. She called out to them to let them know that she was home. With only half an hour to shower and get dressed before Officer Jones came to pick them up, she told Jamie he had to hurry and get out of the shower. Soon, she had the bathroom all to herself. She hurriedly showered and combed her hair. As she was getting dressed, the doorbell rang, signaling Officer Jones' arrival.

Jamie, who was already dressed, ran to the door to let Officer Jones in; he welcomed him and offered him a seat. He said he was a little early but did not mind waiting. Jamie watched as his mother came downstairs; he could see the delight in Officer Jones' eyes as he got up and greeted her with a big smile. Was there also a bit of excitement in their mother's eyes? Maria had followed her mother down, and she had not missed the exchange between the two. They went to the car, and

Officer Jones opened the door for Karla to enter. Maria looked at her brother, and they both exchanged smiles. They were both thinking that Officer Jones really liked their mom, and it seemed that Mom was softening towards the policeman.

It was a short ride to the church. Maria could already see the church in the distance. It appeared that the church parking lot was almost filled, but they were lucky enough to get a spot someone had just pulled out of near the front of the church. Officer Jones jumped out of the car, made his way around to the passengers' side, and opened the door for Karla.

"Thank you, Mark," she giggled.

"It's my pleasure, ma'am," he replied with a small salute as if she were a superior officer.

As they walked towards the church, Maria became lost in thought as she reflected on her father's funeral. *I wonder how the family is coping now that the time has come for the burial.* This was the first funeral they had attended since her father's death. She quickly glanced at her mom and brother to see how they were coping with the memories. Mom was trying her best to keep back the tears, and it appeared that Jamie was trying to be brave for them. Her mind went back to that day, that unbearable day when they said their final goodbyes to their beloved dad. Going to the funeral had certainly brought back memories, sad ones, and she was not sure if she could withstand the tears. She remembered that it was at her father's funeral it had hit home that she would never see him again. How she had cried as reality struck, but her brother had placed his arms around her and reminded her that this was temporary and if she remained faithful to God, she would see their father again. It had made her feel a bit better, but it did not stop the ache and longing in her heart for her beloved father. She could only imagine what Lori's family was going through at that moment in church.

Maria became aware that they had entered the church; she was so deep in thought that she had just followed the group without taking note of her steps. She glanced towards the front to see how Lori and her family were doing. She could see their shoulders shaking with sobs, except for Lori's father, who was staring straight ahead. He appeared to be staring but not seeing. Her mother suggested that they go across and greet the family.

"Just give them a hug," she said. "Sometimes, a hug says more than words could express. What can you say to someone at a time like this?"

"Nothing," replied Officer Jones. Maria had forgotten that he too had experienced tragedy, with not losing just one person but two. *He must be experiencing similar feelings as we are,* she mused. *I guess in life, we all experience sadness one time or another, and every family will experience death.*

They made their way across to the family. There were other people waiting in line to give their condolences, so they joined the line awaiting their turn. The line moved quite quickly, and soon, Maria found herself embracing Lori. Lori clung to her, crying, "Thank you for coming; it means so much to me." Maria responded with a squeeze and told her to call if she needed someone to talk to. Maria's heart went out to Lori; she certainly understood the emotional trauma that would follow this day. The family moved on to find a seat, and Maria sat in the seat closest to the aisle. She glanced across at her mother and Jamie and thought she saw a glimmer of tears in their eyes. This was not easy for any of them, including Officer Jones.

She snapped out of her thoughts when she heard the pastor begin to speak. She stood as they sang but remembered little else of the service until Lori got up to give a tribute to her sister. Maria was all ears, thinking, *How did Lori muster up the strength and courage to do this?* Lori spoke about her sister's personality and her love for life. She portrayed her sister as a delightful, happy child who was gifted in music and math.

"Joanna had an angelic voice and was always singing," Lori said. "She frequently made up the songs she sang. Her songs were happy songs, she made our house come alive with laughter, and she always cheered me up with her funny jokes." Maria could see Lori was trying hard to be brave. Her voice sometimes cracked as she sought to hold back the tears.

As Maria watched and listened, she could feel a lump forming in her throat; this was proving harder than she had anticipated. Her heart broke for Lori, knowing full well what the coming days would be like for the family. She wished the service would be over soon—it brought back too many memories. She had to be strong; she could not let Lori see her tears, tears for Joanna, who had died, tears for Lori and the family, and tears for the loss of her father. Although a year had passed since that fateful day, Maria still carried the memories in her heart. The pain was not as sharp, but it was still there. Will it ever be gone? she asked herself.

Maria watched as Lori went back to sit with her family. Mr. Thomas put his arms around her and hugged her tightly. He whispered something in her ears and gave her a kiss on the cheek. The service came to an end, and the family walked down the aisle. As they passed by Maria, Lori stopped and whispered to her, "Call me; I need to talk." Maria assured her that she would call later that night.

The drive back to the house was silent; no one spoke, each engrossed in their own thoughts. It had not been easy, but they had kept their promise to be there for the Thomas family, and they were. The real challenge for the family would now begin. The service and the burial signaled the finality of death. Now the healing process will start. This is when they would need a friend, a shoulder to cry on, someone to talk to that would have real empathy.

The Rodriquez and the Thomas family kept in touch throughout the rest of the week; Maria and Lori, Karla and Susan, and Jamie and Chris. Officer Jones had also kept in touch with Mr. Thomas. The weekend came to an end, and Lori was expected to return to school that Monday. She had shared with Maria the challenge she felt she would be facing. She had not been able to concentrate on anything since her sister's death and wondered how she would cope with schoolwork and catching up with the work that she had missed. Maria promised to assist her any way she could. This tragedy had resulted in a bond being formed between the two girls, and Maria wondered how that would play out when Brianna and Angie saw that Lori had become her friend.

Chapter 15

Maria was late waking up; she had changed the time on her alarm clock over the weekend and forgot to reset it for Monday. Already she could hear Jamie and Mom downstairs in the kitchen. She went in overdrive as she showered and dressed in record time. She did not want to miss spending time with Jamie and her mom before school. Over the weekend, they had spent a few hours on Saturday with the Thomas family, and on Sunday, Lori had come over for a few hours. Lori was not very open in sharing her feelings, and Maria respected her right to privacy. They spoke of school, and Maria brought her up to date with what they had done in math class. The rest of the conversation was kept to "safe" topics. Maria got to know Lori a little better, but she understood that it would take time for Lori to open and share any significant part of her thoughts and life with her. The time spent with the Thomas family and Lori over the weekend had cut into their weekend family time, so

Maria did not want to miss having breakfast with her family.

"Come down for breakfast, or it's going to be cold," Jamie shouted. Maria ran down the stairs to the aroma of bacon, eggs, and toast. Mom would want her to have a glass of freshly squeezed orange juice with it. *It tasted so much better than the store-bought orange juice,* she thought. She gave her mom and brother a kiss on the cheek in appreciation for preparing breakfast. They caught up on their talking while they ate; all too soon, it was time for Jamie to leave for school. He ran out the door leaving Maria to spend some alone time with her mom. She shared with her mom the concerns she had for Lori and hoped that Brianna and Angie would be sensitive enough to her feelings. The girls in the clique and Lori had not spoken during her absence from school, and Maria had not divulged any information about the breaking up of the clique. She wanted Lori to be free to make her own decisions without any persuasions from her.

"Time to go," Mom said. "It is amazing how time seems to grow wings and fly away when you are having a good time. Love you, honey, have a great day at school."

"Thanks, Mom, love you too," Maria responded. As Maria made her way to the bus stop, her mind went to Lori, and she wondered how she would cope her first day back at school. She was sure some students would want to know why she was absent, and the ones who knew about her sister's death would want to know what really happened. Maria could only wish that everyone would be sensitive to Lori's feelings and not ask too many questions. Then there was Brianna and Angie; what would be their reaction, and would Lori still want to be a part of the clique? Maria just wanted what was best for Lori and hoped she would make the right choice.

"Maria," John called out to her, and on seeing him, she ran towards him and gave him a playful pat on the back. "It's so good to see you, John. I guess your mom could not take you to school this morning, right? Her loss is my gain," she laughed.

"Good to see you too. We can sit together and do some catching up," John responded.

"You have not taken the bus for a few weeks, so you have no idea of the changes that have taken place with me at school. When we see each other in the hallway, we are always in a rush to get to class on time, so we never have time to talk. I'll call and update you when I get home; I don't want to talk about it on the bus."

Terry came up and greeted Maria. "Oh, Terry, this is my friend John, I've known him forever, and our families are very close." The two greeted each other as the bus pulled in at the stop. They boarded the bus; John sat by Maria, and Terry sat across from them. Maria was careful to keep her conversation neutral; she had befriended Terry, but she still did not know her very well. It was better to be careful and not say too much in her presence, at least until she got to know her better. Terry had no clue that Maria had visited Lori and had also attended Joanna's funeral, and she knew Terry was not in touch with Lori outside of school. Maria had a way of holding a conversation with herself in her mind, so her thoughts were on how everything would play out at school that day.

"You're deep in thought," John said.

"I was just thinking about school and what the day would be like. I do not expect any problems, but one never knows," she said under her breath.

"Everything will be fine," John responded. "Just be yourself."

Maria did not expect to have any trouble at school. She had learned to "keep her tongue" and to think before she speaks. As she disembarked the bus, she ran into Jackie, who had just gotten off her bus. John hugged her, and they parted ways as Jackie fell in step with her. She had kept Jackie abreast of some of the events with Lori, but she felt that the more private matters concerning Lori should not be discussed as it would be violating Lori and her family's privacy. She would, however, tell her about the funeral later since Terry had now joined them. The three girls made their way to their math class; they all felt that although Mr. Jones appeared to be harsh, he was a softy on the inside; it was obvious to everyone that he wanted his students to excel. Knowing that he was extremely strict on students reporting to his class late, they hurried along, wanting to get there so they could solve the problems on the whiteboard before the late bell rang for class.

Mr. Jones was standing at the classroom door, and he greeted the girls as they entered the classroom and glanced at them with raised eyebrows. They looked at each other and laughed.

"I think he must be wondering when we all became friends," Jackie said.

"I hope he will have many more surprises when the toxic relationship we have with the rest of the clique is diffused," Maria quipped. "I know there is a better way, and I trust that God will show us how to solve the problem, or He will work it out for us."

Maria and her family had started to attend church again, and she had spent time with her family reading the Bible and praying. *Now, I understand why Daddy was different; it was because of the word that he had hidden in his heart. His life reflected the beauty of Christ. Now, I understand some of the things my father taught me when he was alive,* she thought to herself.

Terry had never heard anyone talk about God like that. She wondered what her newfound friend meant by "God will work it out for us." *I never heard of God working anything out for anyone or helping anyone to solve a problem. I was told that we must make our own choices and work things out ourselves; and that the decisions we make today will affect our future. So how does God come into this?* she wondered. They took their seats, and Maria and Jackie began to work the problems on the board. Terry, on the other hand, was still pondering what God had to do with the problems she faced with her ex-friend. *I must ask Maria what she meant by that statement,* she told herself. She became aware that she had not yet copied the problems from the board, much less solved them, so she redirected her focus to the problem at hand, rushing to complete it before Mr. Jones finished taking the attendance.

Terry completed the problem just as the bell rang. Mr. Jones told the class that from now on, they would only have three minutes to solve the two problems. "I am grooming you for the world of work. Time is important; pay attention, ask questions, focus, do your best, practice working problems at home, be confident in your abilities, then you will be on your way to a successful life."

Terry watched him as he strolled around the classroom, looking at every student's paper. She had never heard him speak like that before, is he going strange on her like Maria? *We're only in middle school, so how could he be grooming us for the world of work? But then again, I never really listened to him, and he does make sense. Maybe I have been missing out on Mr. Jones' words of wisdom all along. I am so happy that my parents gave me an ultimatum, and I got out of that clique,* Terry thought to herself. She became aware that Mr. Jones was indicating to her that she should solve the problem on the whiteboard. She had forgotten that he always selected people who appeared to be distracted, and she certainly had been since she sat down. Terry was happy she could solve the problem and explain the steps to the class.

"Well done, Terry, your explanation was clear," Mr. Jones remarked. By a show of hands, the students indicated that they had all grasped the concept and understood the steps to the problems. Mr. Jones walked around the classroom, glancing at each student's paper to see if they really understood. He stood still by Angie and Brianna's desks and quietly said something to them.

The classroom door opened, and Lori walked in. All eyes turned; there was a hush in the room.

"Welcome back, Lori," Mr. Jones exclaimed. "We missed you. Maria has mastered the areas covered in your absence, so I am assigning her the responsibility of working with you during the breakout session today and for the rest of the week. She will bring you up to date on the areas you have missed. I have prepared a packet for you to work on in class and at home so you can bring your grades up. If you have any difficulty with any of the worksheets, raise your hand, and I'll be over to assist you."

"Thank you, sir," Lori replied as she walked over and sat in her usual seat beside Angie. Angie tried to talk to her, but Lori seemed distant; she did not reply. Mr. Jones proceeded to introduce a new concept while working through a few problems. He divided the class into groups and assigned leaders and tables to each group. He placed Maria and Lori at a table at the back of the room, and Brianna and Angie were assigned a table beside Mr. Jones' desk.

Maria sat by Lori and enquired of her how she was feeling. Lori did not want to talk, so Maria went straight to explaining the new math concepts taught in her absence and worked through a few problems from the text to give Lori a better understanding of how to solve them. Maria guided her as she solved the first problem and watched her solve the second. Lori indicated that she understood and wanted to complete the worksheets she had missed. She then proceeded to work on those that Mr. Jones had assigned for that day, while Maria proceeded to work on the problems for that day. She whispered to Lori, "I'm here for you if you feel like talking." She wrote her telephone number and passed it to Lori, "Call me if you need to talk." Lori took the paper, thanked her, and continued to work on the assignment.

Not long after, Mr. Jones pulled the class back together, reviewed what was taught, and gave them a problem to work on. "You have five minutes to the bell; hand me the solution to the problem on your way out. Lori, you are exempt from this assignment; continue to work on the package I gave you. If you have completed the page I assigned for today, detach it from the package and hand it in on your way out."

The bell sounded; the students gathered their belongings and handed in the assignment on their way out the door. Maria asked Lori if she wanted her to accompany her to her next class, but she refused. She wanted to be alone. Maria understood the thoughts and emotions that Lori was experiencing and that it would take time for Lori to get to the place where she was comfortable talking about her emotions. She had been there, so had Jackie. She watched the conflicting emotions on Jackie's face as she watched Lori walk away. It was difficult to lose a loved one and watch others laugh, talk, and have fun when your heart was breaking. She wished Lori could see that they understood the pain, hurt, and emptiness she was feeling and that they could help her through the healing process.

If they could just leave me alone to grieve, I want to be left alone. Lori's heart was aching, and she felt empty. Life somehow had lost its appeal. *I miss my sister so much,* she thought, as she walked lifelessly to class. Every step was hard, *If I could only curl up and die, then all this would be over. I love my parents and my brother, but Joanna, she was special, we were very close, and I miss her laughter. I know my family loves me, and they would be devastated if something should happen to me, so I better snap out of this and focus on what is at hand.*

As she entered the classroom, she was greeted by Miss Mason, her science teacher, who hugged her. They said nothing to each other, but the embrace made Lori feel a little better. It communicated to her that she empathized with her; the gesture meant more to her than if she had said something.

Lori went through the rest of the day as if she were in another world, looking but not seeing, hearing but not listening. *Whoever says coping with the death of a loved one is easy knows nothing about trauma,* she thought. The final bell for the day sounded, and Lori made her way to the parent pick-up area. Her father had told her he would take her to school and pick her up every day until she felt comfortable enough to ride the bus again. The tragedy had brought about a change in her father. He was not so absorbed in his work; he was spending time with his family. *Look what it had to take for him to realize that we needed him. If he had only taken Joanna to school as Mom asked him to, she would be here now.* Lori felt bitterness and anger seeping into her mind, and she did not want to go there. *What use would that do?* she asked herself. *Dad was hurting just as much, if not even more than the rest of the family; he blamed himself for Joanna's death.* She felt like she blamed him too, but she had to get past that. If the family were to heal, they all had to forgive; she had to forgive her dad.

Lori could see her dad's car in the line as it slowly moved towards the pick-up area. She wanted to be a little cheerful for him, but it did not make sense, so she faked it. He would see right through her. As he pulled up to where she was standing, she could see the pain in his eyes. *He must have had as bad a day as I did,* she thought to herself. She got in the car, and her dad asked her about her day.

"Not good," she responded.

"Neither was mine," her father replied. "It is difficult, but we will make it if we support each other. Can you forgive me? I have a hard time forgiving myself, but I know in my heart that I must if I am to heal."

Lori was quiet for some time, then she said, "Yes, Dad, I forgive you, and we will heal together. Remember, she was with me when this happened, and I sometimes blame myself too. We couldn't help it, Dad, and we must stop blaming ourselves and each other."

"Thanks, Lori; maybe we could take the Rodriquez family up on their offer. You could call Maria and talk with her, and I will discuss this with your mother and brother to see if they would want to accept the help that was offered to us. I will contact Officer Jones; maybe he could help me."

"That is a good idea, Dad. Maria gave me her number today. I will give her a call because I need someone to talk to. She seems a nice girl." She paused. "Dad, do you know I have been very mean to Maria in the past? I hang out with a group of girls who have been very unkind to several students, and Maria is one of them. I was not even aware that she had lost her father a year ago. I cannot imagine what she must have gone through coping with the death of her father and the bullying she received from our group at school. Yet, she was able to show me kindness. I don't understand it; there is just something different about her," Lori explained, looking sober.

"You know, there is something different about the whole family. They have shown us kindness when all they got from me at the beginning was harassment. Lori, we all make mistakes, and many times we lack good judgment," he replied and then shared with her the episode when he trailed Maria and threatened her.

"Dad, you did not."

"Yes, I did, and I am very ashamed of myself. I apologized to the family, and they were very gracious, so you see, you are not the only one who made poor decisions. I allowed my emotions to get the best of me, and I reacted without thinking it through. What I did was inexcusable; I sure caused Maria a lot of fear and grief. We are home; let us see what your mom is doing."

Susan was in the kitchen preparing dinner. From her gait, Jack saw how dejected and sad she was. Life without Joanna was certainly taking a toll on her. Preparing dinner was a special time for Susan and Joanna; they had spent many days together talking and laughing as Susan prepared dinner. Joanna asked many questions, and Mom would jokingly tell her she asked too many questions. "I would give anything to hear her ask me questions again," Susan whispered under her breath.

Lori overheard the comment and suggested to her mother that she wait until she got home to prepare dinner so they could spend some time together in the kitchen. "I know I have not been too kind lately," Lori remarked. "But I would like us to spend more time together, even if it means me learning to cook. You never know; I may actually like it."

"Oh, that would be nice, Lori. I'd love that," Susan answered.

"Let me wash my hands and help you in the kitchen, Mom."

"Thanks, dear."

As Lori washed her hands, she reflected on the past year and concluded that she had spent most of her time in her room, on the phone texting her friends, or watching television and had not spent time with her family. She decided she would begin to spend more time with her brother and her parents because they were all she had, and they needed each other. *We will get through this,* she muttered.

"Mom, what can I help you with?" Lori asked as she came into the kitchen.

"I'm almost finished, so you could put the place settings on the table and get the serving dishes. It has been a long time since we sat at the dinner table as a family. Your dad and I have decided that, because we have missed out on so much of your children growing up, we should make every effort to have dinner together every day."

"We could use that time to hear about your day and the challenges and joys of school life. It is always good for families to share their hearts, and sharing a meal together is a good place to start. Maybe we can learn a bit more about your dad's job; sharing keeps us up to date as to what is happening in each other's life."

"That's exciting, Mom."

"Now, dinner is ready, so I'll put the serving dishes on while you go upstairs and let your dad and brother know that dinner is served."

Lori ran upstairs to call her dad and brother to dinner. Dad thanked Susan for preparing the meal and complimented her on how delicious it looked.

"I'm sure that it tastes even better than how it looks," Jack remarked.

Susan responded with a slight smile. Sitting down to a meal together felt a bit strange to the kids; they could not remember the last time they had eaten together as a family. Jack tried hard to engage the children in a conversation. Lori joined in, but Chris had a hard time sharing. Eventually, they all warmed up to his efforts. They began to share a little about their day and how they were feeling. Mom joined in, encouraging everyone to talk about the things that troubled them and the things that they enjoyed doing. Although the conversations did not flow smoothly, and there were times of awkward silence, Dad felt that progress was made and expressed his confidence that the family would rise from tragedy to triumph as they learned to cherish each other and value every moment they spent together.

"Lori and I, on our way home, discussed taking up the invitation of the Rodriquez family to call them when we need to talk. I think it is a good idea for Chris to call Jamie, Lori to talk to Maria, and Susan to call Karla. I will call Officer Jones when I feel I need someone to talk to or when I feel overwhelmed. How do you feel about that, Susan and Chris?"

They responded that they were not sure they were ready to talk to anyone in detail about their feelings but would consider doing so if they found they were not coping well.

"I am going to call Maria tonight; she gave me her telephone number today, and I really need to share with someone who has experienced the loss of a family member. I think she will help me to face my feelings, accept that Joanna is gone, and move forward in the healing process."

"That's great, Lori," her dad replied. "Chris and I will take care of the kitchen, Susan. You must be very tired, plus this will give me an opportunity to spend time with Chris to get to know him better, a time to bond with each other. Lori, you go make your call to Maria."

Chris was surprised that his father wanted to spend time with him; how he had longed for his fathers' attention. He quickly put aside the thoughts that played in his head that his father was to blame for Joanna's death. *Blaming Dad cannot bring Joanna back,* he reminded himself. It was sad that it took tragedy to bring about a change in his father, but Dad had reached out to him, and he would seize the opportunity to spend time with him. *Maybe, just maybe, we will get to know each other better.*

Chapter 16

"Maria, your phone is ringing," Karla called from the living room.

Maria ran downstairs to answer the phone. She was a bit surprised to hear Lori's voice on the other end of the line. Although she had given Lori her telephone number, she was not sure she would have taken her up on her offer. Maria, sensing that Lori was still a bit hesitant to share, led the conversation into safe topics such as classes, her day at school, things she enjoyed doing, and eventually encouraging her to talk about her emotions. Maria got to know Lori better and discovered that they had quite a few things in common. They both loved nature; they loved to walk in the park and enjoyed watching the various animals, birds, and insects there. Lori also loved to take pictures of nature and had a large collection of photographs she had taken. Based on Lori's description of her photos, Maria concluded that she had built quite an impressive portfolio. Lori had enlarged and hung her favorite photos on her bedroom wall.

"I would love to be able to view your collection of photographs," Maria said.

"Maybe on the weekend you could come over, and I will show you my portfolio."

"I am certainly looking forward to that," Maria replied.

"Maria, the real reason I called you is that I feel so numb, I miss my sister very much, and I need someone to talk to. You understand what it feels like to have lost someone you love, and for it to happen suddenly makes it harder to bear. I feel you must have experienced some of the same emotions that I am feeling. I feel the need to pour out my feelings to someone who understands."

Maria and Lori spent hours on the phone talking. Maria did more listening than talking; from experience, she knew that if Lori could talk about the tragedy, it would help her in the healing process. She gave advice only when it was asked of her. Lori thanked Maria and told her that she felt better having shared her feelings with her.

"There are going to be times when you will feel the same way you did earlier on," Maria responded. "But this is natural, do not be discouraged when this happens. The healing process takes time."

"Thanks, Maria. I am so sorry that I made your life uncomfortable in the past. Can you forgive me?"

"Why not? Consider yourself forgiven," Maria replied.

"Thanks again. See you tomorrow."

Lori lay in bed thinking about the events of the day. On the surface, things appeared to have gone well, but no one knew the turmoil she had undergone internally throughout the day. Maybe Maria understood, but she doubted anyone else did. She lay awake thinking about her sister and how much she missed her. She was getting to accept the fact that her sister would never be coming home again. *No one is ever prepared for a loved one's death; it is just something that springs up out of nowhere and takes you by surprise, leaving you in a tailspin, she thought. I would not wish this to happen to anyone, and I certainly hope this never happens to my family again. I do not know how I could survive another tragedy.*

She pulled herself out of the depressive thoughts and decided that she would begin to be grateful that she had parents and a brother who loved her, and she had a decent family life. Things had certainly begun to change in her family; they were talking and spending more time with each other. Out of Joanna's passing had come some good, but what a price to pay, the death of her sister. *I need to stop looking at the past and focus on the future; what happened cannot be reversed. The future can be great, and I intend to do the best for Joanna's memory and myself. Although she is gone, I will make her proud of me.* She slid beneath the covers, telling herself she needed to sleep so she would be alert in school. *I am going to have a better day at school tomorrow, and I will do everything to bring my grades up.*

She woke to a knock on her door; it was her mom telling her that breakfast was almost ready, so she needed to come down. Lori was always good on time, she rarely overslept, but she had laid awake for so long that it was almost two in the morning before she fell asleep. She quickly showered, got dressed, and ran downstairs; she wanted to have breakfast with the family and not keep her dad waiting to take her to school. Again, she felt gratitude for the change in her family; she began to feel loved and that her feelings and her opinions mattered. The rest of the family was already seated at the breakfast table; they were all waiting for her to come down before they started eating. She apologized for her lateness and sat down. Her dad proceeded to pray before the meal; although in the past they had visited a church a few times, she did not remember ever hearing her dad pray before, much less thank God for a meal. She wanted to know more about God because she had seen how different Maria was from the other students, and in talking to her, she knew that Maria attended church and prayed. *Maybe, just maybe, she thought, we can be like that family. They seem to be happy even after their tragedy.*

Chris had opted to continue taking the bus, but Lori accepted her dad's invitation to take her to and from school until she felt comfortable taking the bus again. She had enjoyed the ride with her dad yesterday because it gave them the opportunity to spend time together and get to know each other better. As she sat in the car, the annoying thought popped into her mind again, *Look what it took for me to spend time with my dad. I will not allow those thoughts to come into my mind,* she said to herself. Lori decided that she would prefer to spend the time in profitable conversation than to spend it on negative thoughts. She and her dad chatted about school, and he encouraged her to do her best. As he pulled to a stop at school, Lori gave him a hug and wished him a good day. She opened the car door to come out, then paused and whispered, "Dad, I'm going to do my best to keep focused on school. I know I can talk to Maria if I begin to feel sad; she knows how to encourage me and make me feel better. Thanks, Dad. I love you, have a great day."

"Bye, Lori. I love you too, and remember I'm always proud of you," her dad replied.

Lori walked slowly to class. She had completed two days' work in math and had worked on assignments for her other classes. She was deep in thought when she bumped into someone. On looking up, she saw Angie and Brianna. She felt they had seen her and deliberately stood in her way; she knew how they operated and had decided she would not be a party to their destructive behaviors anymore.

"I noticed yesterday you did not speak to any of us, but we saw you with our archenemy, Maria. Are you one of us or not?" Angie stated.

Lori looked at them both and declared, "I lost my sister, you did not even ask me how I felt, but you come to talk to me about not speaking to you yesterday. You are both selfish and cruel. You disgust me, you are not anyone's friend, and I certainly will not be a part of your clique anymore. I don't know how I could have fallen for your schemes; I chose to partake in your cruel jokes about other people, and I dislike myself for that, but I will not stoop to such behavior again and will not dumb myself down so you can feel good about yourself," Lori answered angrily.

Angie and Brianna were taken by surprise. They never knew Lori had it in her to stand up for herself; they saw her as weak and a pawn in their hands. They thought they could bully her, and she would be frightened and turn her back on Maria. What they did not understand was that in adversity, a person could sink or swim. Lori had chosen to swim. She had taken that adversity and turned it around to build her character and her strength. It had changed her outlook on life; she had become a better person because of the tragedy, and she was not going to let anyone take that from her. She walked off, leaving them with their mouths wide open in disbelief. They were utterly stunned. She thought how different Maria was from Angie and Brianna and decided she would thank Maria and her family for all they had done to help her family. *She really is a nice girl. I would like to hang out with her and her friends because they focus on their schoolwork, they are kind to others, and they would impact me positively. The school year is more than halfway through, but I can turn my grades and my life around.*

Lori continued to class; she felt proud of herself for having stood up to the two bullies and was glad that Terry had removed herself from the clique. The clique was being dismantled, and she was happy she was not a part of it anymore.

Chapter 17

Maria and Terry met up with Jackie on their way to class. They were early for class, and Mr. Jones told them instead of standing at the door, they should go in and sit in the classroom. They were soon joined by Lori and a few other students. As Lori entered the classroom, she greeted the three girls, chatted a little with them, and went to her usual seat. She was determined that she would not ask for her seat to be changed; she would sit beside Angie and Brianna but not be a part of their awful drama. She wanted to prove to herself that she could focus and not be distracted by the negative behavior of others. She felt a bit sorry for them because the group had dwindled to two persons. Although she had decided she would not be a part of the clique anymore, she felt she could be a positive influence in their lives. She was determined to show them the same type of kindness that Maria showed her even after she had treated her so badly. *I do not think Maria understands the impact she has had on my life and the life of my family. I hope my behavior will encourage others to change in the same way Maria has helped me,* she thought.

The day went uneventful. Lori still faced challenges, but she remembered the encouragement Maria had given her, and she kept refocusing. Angie and Brianna kept making comments under their breath, but Lori did not allow this to distract her one bit. She sat with Maria for part of the breakout session as Maria brought her up to date with the rest of the assignments she had missed. Then, she diligently worked through the package Mr. Jones had given her. There were times when sadness seemed to overcome her, but Maria and the other two girls had walked her to all her classes and kept encouraging her. Unknown to her, they had received permission from the principal to walk her to each of her classes, and they were given late passes. That had helped her quite a bit. Lori's resolution was strengthened; she would seek to help others who might face similar situations like hers because of the kindness shown to her by Maria and her family.

The last bell of the day sounded, and Lori walked to the car pick-up area. Her father was already there. She greeted him as she climbed into the car. He wanted to know all about her day, so she chatted the entire way home. She told her father about her classes, her inner struggles, and how Maria and the other girls had encouraged her.

"By the way, Dad, I stood up to Angie and Brianna today; you would have been proud of me."

"I am always proud of you, sweetheart, and I hope that one day you will be proud of me too."

"Dad, you know I love you, and I am proud of your accomplishments; you have become more loving and caring, and I cherish our time together. Thanks for being there for me. I invited Maria over to the house this evening to see my photography portfolio. I hope it is okay because I did not check with you or Mom first."

"That is a great idea, and I am sure your mom will be happy to have her over. She is a good influence for you."

"Maria has not confirmed if she will come over; she will ask her mom's permission and let me know. I hope Mrs. Rodriquez will allow her to come; I really like spending time with her," Lori stated.

Maria got home before her mom. Jamie had kept his word and was already preparing dinner. She greeted Jamie, put her bag down, and informed him that she was going up to take a shower and would be back down to set the dining table. As Maria came down the stairs, her mom came through the front door. Jamie had informed her that dinner was almost ready, so Maria quickly put the place settings on the table. The three of them chatted through the final stages of preparation and sat down to eat. Their mother asked Jamie to grace the table and thank God for His provisions, after which they proceeded to eat. Mrs. Rodriquez had to go to her second job, so they did not have much time together at the dinner table.

"Mom, Lori invited me over this evening to look at some nature photographs she has taken. She said she loves nature, and capturing scenes is her passion. Is it okay for me to visit her? I will be back by seven."

"You can go if your brother will walk you back home when you are done visiting."

"I am going to play basketball with my friends, but I will come over and walk you back home by seven."

"Thanks to you, Mom and Jamie. I will call Lori after dinner and let her know I'll be over."

After the family finished dinner, Maria washed the dishes and cleaned the kitchen, then settled down to complete her homework. She only had science homework, which she completed within the hour. She called Lori to let her know that her mother had agreed for her to come over and that her brother would pick her up at seven. "I'll be over in about thirty minutes."

Lori was excited that Maria was able to visit; she looked forward to showing Maria her photographs. "See you soon," Lori responded.

Maria set off with a brisk walk as she looked forward to viewing the pictures. After all, they were of nature, and this was one of her favorite pastimes. She loved outdoors, watching animals, birds, and insects, and admiring the various flowers and trees. Maybe she and Lori could go on nature walks in the park and go hiking someday. She knew her mother would not allow them to go alone, so she would have to try and get Jamie on board. Or maybe both families could go. The big question she asked within herself was, is Lori's family into nature the way her family enjoys it? *Well enough of that,* she said to herself as she turned in the gate. She proceeded to ring the doorbell. The door opened quickly; Lori was by the window watching out for her.

"Glad you were able to come! I'm so excited to show you my portfolio."

"I'm looking forward to viewing it too."

"Come on in; Mom is baking bread and cupcakes. I love the smell of freshly baked bread, and I love eating it hot with butter. You will enjoy it; Mom makes the best cupcakes ever."

"I bet she does. I love the smell and taste of fresh bread, too," Maria responded.

Maria greeted Mrs. Thomas and thanked her for having her over.

"It's a pleasure, Maria; you have helped our family in many ways. You can come over anytime you want, and Lori is free to visit you if your mom is in agreement."

"Thank you, I'm sure my mom will be okay with that," Maria assured her.

Mrs. Thomas was quiet for a while, then remarked, "You know, I usually do not allow Lori to have any friends over or visit her friends' homes, but you and your family are different. You are a positive role model for her, she likes you, and she needs a good and loyal friend."

"Thanks, Mrs. Thomas, but you know I also had my struggles, and I used to respond in a negative way to Lori and her friends, but I learned a better way. When I got angry, my dad would say to me, 'Pumpkin, remember, a soft answer turneth away wrath, but grievous words stir up anger.'"

"At first, I had no idea what he meant by those words, and I never asked him, but when things got rough at school, I thought a lot about those words, and I think I am beginning to understand. I put them into practice by thinking about positive ways to respond to others when I felt as if they had hurt me, and it changed my outlook on life. Do you know that it is in the Bible?"

"I am sorry, but I have stopped reading the Bible a long time ago; I will get back to it. I grew up in the church, so I know many Bible verses. Thank you for reminding me of the importance of staying in the Word."

Mr. Thomas and Chris came downstairs and greeted Maria. "Good to see you, Maria. Lori told me she invited you over to view her photographs. If I may say so myself, they are pretty impressive," Mr. Thomas said.

"Thank you, sir. I'm looking forward to seeing them myself."

"Let's go look at my photos, Maria, before it's time for Jamie to pick you up."

Lori and Maria ran upstairs. Maria gasped in amazement as Lori's room was full of her photos hanging on the wall. They were beautiful. Maria walked around the room, taking in the photos one by one; she could not believe her eyes. Lori had captured the minutest detail; she had the gift of spotting the perfect picture and capturing it with her lens.

Lori also had a huge portfolio which she kept in a specially locked cabinet her father had bought her. "I kept these locked away to prevent Joanna from pulling them out and looking at them every day. I wanted to protect them because they were my best shots. Had I known that she would be gone so soon, I would have allowed her to keep looking at them. I wouldn't have cared."

Lori became silent; Maria knew she needed a moment to gather herself, so she kept quiet until Lori asked the question, "Do you think I am a bad person for locking up my photographs?"

"Oh no, it is perfectly natural to want to protect your photos, even from people you love. Do not go back to the past; it is gone. Instead, look to the future. You have a very prosperous future ahead of you. You will always miss Joanna, and she will always be a part of your life, but do not blame yourself; it will only make you depressed. Go out and be a success for her."

"Thanks, Maria, you always know how to encourage me. Let us look at the photos in my portfolio. I do not think we will have time to look at all of them." The girls shared their thoughts about each photo and chatted about their love for nature. They discovered they had a lot in common and vowed to spend more time together outside of school. This would be easy because they lived near each other. All too soon, the doorbell rang; they were enjoying themselves so much they had not realized the time had sped by so quickly it was six fifty and Jamie had come to walk Maria home.

Lori hugged Maria, "Thanks for coming over; it meant a lot to me."

"I enjoyed myself too," Maria responded. The girls ran downstairs. Jamie was talking to Chris, so they sat and waited. Chris asked if he could give Jamie a call later because he needed to talk to someone. Jamie agreed and said that eight o'clock would be fine. As Jamie and Maria said goodbye to the family, Mrs. Thomas gave them a loaf of bread and some cupcakes to take home. The kids thanked her and turned to leave when Mr. Thomas offered them a ride home. "I'll come with you, Dad," Lori chirped in.

"Okay, sweetheart."

The kids accepted, and they all piled in the car. The journey was short, and they got there in a few minutes. Maria and Jamie thanked Mr. Thomas for the ride. He waited until they were inside before he and Lori drove off. Maria could see Lori waving goodbye through the window.

"Life is unpredictable," Jamie remarked. "That is why we have to cherish each moment."

Chapter 18

Maria jumped out of bed as her alarm clock sounded. She felt well-rested and ready for the day. School seemed more appealing these days. Maria whispered to herself, "I am enjoying my time at school." Things had changed for the better, and she had gained three new friends, Jackie, Terry, and Lori. She did not think she would gain the friendship of either Brianna or Angie, but she hoped they could at least be civil with each other. Maria was convinced that underneath the tough exterior lay two broken, wounded girls. "I wonder what their lives are like," Maria whispered to herself. "I may never know, but I will be kind to them," she promised herself.

She could hear Jamie in the shower, so she quickly made her bed and grabbed her clothes in preparation for her shower. She took the opportunity to check if she had put her assignments in her bag, closed it, and uttered a word of prayer. By then, Jamie had come out of the bathroom; she could hear his door shut. She showered and made her way downstairs to help with breakfast. Mom was already there, and they all decided they would have fruit, a hot drink, and toast or cereal. Maria decided she would have cereal, and she would cut up a banana in it. She chose to have almond milk instead of regular milk; she thought that was one of the best breakfasts ever, except for toast, bacon, and eggs. Mom and Jamie decided on an apple, marmalade with toast, and coffee. Maria brought her mother up to date on her visit with Lori, and Jamie told them he had a productive talk with Chris. He did not give any details, just like a man would do. Maria sighed. Dad was like that; whatever was shared with him was held in confidence unless the person gave permission to share.

Jamie left for school, and Karla and Maria spent time together. All too soon, it was time to go catch the bus. Maria kissed her mother goodbye and made her way to the bus stop. She could see John in the distance—he was riding the bus again today. Maria had not had the opportunity to bring John up to date on all that had taken place, and she promised herself that she would take the time to do so. John had been a true friend to her, and she could not forget John and his mother's kindness to their family during her mom's illness and after the scare she had on her way to school. Maria's mom, Karla, had kept in touch with her friend Mary, and Maria was sure she had kept Mary informed.

"Hey, Maria, good to see you," John called to her.

"It's great to see you too, John. I didn't keep my promise to call you, but we have a little time before the bus comes, so I will bring you up to date on school." Maria gave John a brief update of all that had transpired at school since she last saw him. He told her he was proud of her and encouraged her to continue being a light in school. The bus pulled up to the stop, and the kids climbed on. Terry boarded the bus after John and Maria were seated; she greeted them and sat down two seats behind them. It was a pleasant ride, not too much noise, and few students were talking; most of them were in their own world, some with their headphones on, some texting, and others sleeping. Maria and John seemed to be the only ones on the bus that were talking. Soon, the bus pulled into the bus loop, and the students piled off the bus. John went to his class while Maria waited for Terry to join her. They chatted all the way to the classroom. Mr. Jones was not in his classroom, so they waited with a group of students for him to come. He came just as the bell for classes sounded. By then, Lori and Jackie had joined them, and Brianna and Angie were standing together, a little distance apart. Maria looked across at them and smiled; their response was to contort their faces and turn their backs.

There was less drama in class since Lori and Terry had exited the group. Maria felt sorry for the two girls, who seemed a bit lost since the split. This did not prevent them from some of their antics: they kept up with the name-calling, although it had diminished quite a bit. Maria wondered how she could make a difference in their lives and suggested to her friends that they be courteous to them and not allow themselves to be drawn into any altercation with Angie or Brianna.

After math class, the girls walked together to classes; they would separate when they got to the second floor. On their way, they talked about Brianna and Angie; Maria asked them if they had noticed that each day the "wall" the girls had built around themselves appeared to be breaking down.

"We only have a few weeks before final exams and the end of the school year. I hope we will be able to help them before we leave for summer break." She encouraged her friends to be kind to them and ignore their negative behaviors and comments.

"No one knows what causes people to behave the way they do, and no one knows the challenges people face," Terry remarked.

"Let's get to class before we are marked late," said Maria.

The girls hurried to their respective classes. They bid each other farewell as Maria and Terry entered Miss Lewis' classroom. The rest of the day went well and, soon, they were on their way home.

Chapter 19

Mark could not stop thinking about Karla, but he knew he had to give her time and space to heal before he approached her for a date. Her husband had only been dead for a year, and she needed to do things in her own time. It may be too early for her to even think about someone else; plus, she did not seem to be interested in him. It had taken him five years to come to grips with the fact that his wife and unborn child would not be part of his life anymore, and until now, he had no interest in filling the void that was left after his wife and child died. He never thought he would be interested in anyone again, but Karla was different; she was special, just like how Jane was special but in a different way. From the first moment he saw Karla, he was attracted to her; this was out of the norm for him. He hoped that one day she would allow herself to fall in love again, and it would be with him. He would wait on her.

He glanced at his watch; surprised that time had gone by so quickly, he hopped out of bed and rushed to get dressed. He had been daydreaming about Karla again, and now he was running late for church. Mark had only been a member of the church for six months when Jan, the choir director, discovered quite by accident that Mark had a lovely voice. She heard him singing in the foyer of the church. He came in early and was not aware that anyone was in the choir room. She invited him to audition for the choir, and he was accepted. Although he was not able to attend church regularly because of his job, he endeavored to attend all the choir rehearsals. Last week, his job schedule was changed due to promotion, so now he had weekends off. He shared this information with Jan at the choir rehearsals last Wednesday, and she asked him to sing solo the verses of the song "Great is Thy Faithfulness." The choir would join in with the chorus. *I cannot be late*, he said to himself as he ran out the door.

The Rodriquez and the Thomas family developed a strong relationship, and they felt comfortable sharing freely about their families and beliefs. Jack and Susan Thomas had invited Maria and her family over for dinner on Saturday. They were interested to know more about the Rodriquez family and what made them so different from most of the families they knew. Karla shared with them the love of Christ, His faithfulness to them, and how they had experienced peace even during the storms of life. She told them, if they so desired, they too could have that peace. She took the opportunity to invite them to church on Sunday, and they accepted the invitation to attend.

"Karla, we can pick you up for church, I have a minivan which seats eight people, so there is space for both our families," Jack said.

"What time does your church start?" Susan inquired.

"It starts at eleven, but we try to be there by ten thirty, so we can get a good seat."

"Okay, we'll pick you up at ten fifteen."

"Thank you, Susan," Karla said appreciatively.

Maria got up early on Sunday morning; she was excited that Lori and her family were coming to church with them. She ran downstairs to help her mom prepare breakfast. She wanted to be ready when the Thomases picked them up for church. During breakfast, the family discussed the awesomeness of God and how He had brought the two families together. He had turned a foe into a friend while meeting the needs of each family. They still did not understand why their loved ones died, but they could see how He brought good out of tragedy. "Let us get ready; we only have forty-five minutes before Jack and his family arrive to pick us up," Mom said.

Jack pulled up at exactly ten fifteen. Maria, who was looking out the window, saw the vehicle enter the driveway and informed her mom and Jamie. The families greeted each other as Karla and the kids entered the minivan. The ride was short; soon, they were at church. Jack had plenty of parking spaces to choose from—the benefit of being early. The parking lot began to fill up quickly, and the families took their seats in one of the front pews of the church. Music was playing, and people were filling in as musicians took their seats. Soon, the piped music would be turned off, the praise band would begin to play, and the praise team would lead the congregation into praise and worship. Maria explained to Lori the sequence of the service; she had not been to church in a very long time, and this would be a little strange to her.

The church became quiet as the pastor entered. The praise team took the platform, the band started to play, the praise team began to sing, the people stood up, and worship began. Karla explained to Jack and Susan that they could sing along as the words appeared on the screen. Chris and Lori had never experienced anything like this; they could not understand why people were closing their eyes, raising their hands, and singing to a God they could not even see. But there was a sense of peace throughout the church, and the children could feel that the atmosphere had changed during the singing. They looked at each other, then at Jamie and Maria, and noticed that they too were engrossed in the songs. Their mom and dad were not singing, but they had their eyes closed, and they could see a tear running down their mom's face. Why was their mother crying?

Both Jack and Susan grew up in the church, but they had stopped going to church shortly after the kids were born. Jack had become so engrossed in his work and sought after financial success and validation in his job that he lost all interest in church. Susan was angry that Jack seemed to be more interested in making money than in spending time with the family that she had become angry, blaming God for her problems. She did not realize how much she had missed the fellowship she had at church. She had pulled away from her church family, shut out her friends, and became engrossed in her problems. Jack also realized how much he missed the times he used to spend at church and the friends he had made there. He vowed to himself that this was the beginning of a new chapter in their lives, and he would be an example to his family.

The worship period ended, everyone sat down, the pastor prayed, and the congregation sang. After the Scripture was read, the choir got up to sing, and Mark stepped out to the front and took the microphone.

"Isn't that Officer Mark Jones, Mom?" Maria asked.

"It sure looks like him, but I have never seen him in church before, much less him singing on the choir and a solo part at that."

At the same time, Mark looked up and saw Karla and her family; he looked as if he had seen a ghost. He was equally in shock. He wondered if he would make a fool of himself in front of Karla. The music began, and Mark belted out, "Great is thy faithfulness, oh, God my Father, there is no shadow of turning with thee." For Karla, it was as if time stood still; Mark had such a beautiful voice, and he sang with feeling and expression. The choir joined in the chorus after each verse, but Karla was lost in thought. She was thinking of the words of the song and how great, faithful, and wonderful God had been to them.

The pastor preached on "Letting go of past hurts and mistakes and taking hold of the wonderful future God has in store for us." He quoted the Scripture from Jeremiah 29:11, stating, "'For I know the plans I have for you,' declares the Lord, 'plans to prosper you and not to harm you, plans to give you hope and a future'" (Jeremiah 29:11, NIV). He explained in detail what that verse meant and gave stories of people in the Bible who overcame adversity. Soon they were standing to sing the closing song. Lori remained seated; she was deep in thoughts, and she did not understand some of the things the pastor had spoken about and wanted to know more. She hoped that Maria could explain to her the things she had difficulty understanding. The pastor closed in prayer, and people started to file out of the church, others stood around talking, and Karla introduced Jack and Susan to a few people.

Mark made his way through the crowd to where Karla and the others were standing. He greeted them with, "I had no idea you all came to this church; I was so surprised to see you sitting in the pews."

"I had stopped coming after my husband died, but after I became ill and I scaled back on my job, we started coming again," Karla replied.

"This is the first time for Jack, Susan, and their family; we came together. Mark, I have never seen you in church or singing in the choir before, so how come you are there today and singing a solo part at that?"

Mark explained to them why they had not seen him before and how he came to be singing the solo part.

"You have a wonderful voice, Mark, and I could tell you were singing from your heart. I felt that we were really praising God for His faithfulness," said Karla.

The church was almost empty, as most of the people had left.

"Why don't you all come over to my house at four for dinner?" Susan suggested.

"Thank you, that would be nice, Susan. I'll bake a cake and bring along," Karla agreed.

"Can you bake the same chocolate cake that you gave us? It was really tasty."

"Oh, sure, Susan, no problem," Karla replied.

"The invitation was for you also, Officer Jones."

"Thank you, Susan; I will be there. Karla, I can give you a ride if that's okay with you."

"Thanks, Mark, that is so kind of you."

Lori and Maria were excited. She felt Lori could show her the rest of her portfolio after they had dinner. They chatted all the way to the car; they were home in a short time. Karla changed her clothes and went into the kitchen to start preparing the cakes.

"I'll help you bake the cakes, Mom," Maria offered.

"Thank you, Maria; that would be a great help, honey."

"Sorry I can't help you, Mom; I want to finish my homework before we go," Jamie said.

Karla decided to make three cakes, one for each house; she had to hurry so they would be cool enough for the frosting to be applied. By the time they completed the task in the kitchen, it was time for them to get dressed for dinner.

Mark reflected on the turn of events. Who could think that he would see Karla, her family, and Jack and his family at church? It was wonderful that Karla attended the same church as he did. It was even more amazing to see the two families become friends. With all that had transpired between them, it did not seem very likely. God has a way of turning the tide. He brought good out of something bad. Also, he got to see Karla again, and he was even picking her up to take to dinner. *This is destiny,* he thought.

Mark left on time to pick up Karla and her kids. He came out of the car to greet Karla and to put the cake in the car; he opened the door for her to enter and then went to the driver's seat. The drive was a pleasant one, and the Thomas family was ready and waiting for them. The table was tastefully decorated, and the place settings were gorgeous. Susan and Lori had prepared the dinner, and the aroma of food filled the house. One could smell the tantalizing fragrance of a good pot roast with potatoes. They were shown their places at the dining table, they sat down, and Jack gave thanks for the food. It was a pleasant meal with a lot of chatter. The kids were immersed in conversation, Jamie with Chris and Lori with Maria. The adults were having their own conversation. Karla complimented Susan and Lori on the wonderful meal and then offered to assist in clearing the table. The girls told their moms that they would clear the table and do the dishes before going to Lori's room to look at the rest of her photographs. That would give the parents and Officer Jones time to get to know each other better, plus Lori had questions about the service she wanted to ask Maria.

Jamie and Chris decided they would go outside by the pool and talk. "I have so many questions that I don't know where to start," Chris said.

"It is still difficult for me to sleep well; I stay up at night thinking about Joanna. I sat in church today and wondered if God were so good, how could He have allowed Joanna to die like that? If He is love, is this the way He shows it? You tell me why I should trust Him. Joanna was the light in this house; why did He take her away from us?"

"Chris, I don't claim to have all the answers. All I know is God is good; He does not give us tragedy, the devil does, but He can turn a tragedy into triumph. His word in John 10:10 says the thief, meaning Satan, comes to steal, and to kill, and to destroy, but Jesus Christ has come that we might have life and have it more abundantly. Will you allow Him to heal your heart?"

"If He came to give us life, why did He allow Satan to take my sister's life? What good could come out of that?" Chris sobbed.

"I can't answer that question, Chris. All I know is He loves you, He loved Joanna, and He knows best. Just talk to Him as you are talking to me right now, tell Him how you feel, tell Him of your disappointments and hurts, and ask Him to help you to heal. He wants to have a relationship with you," Jamie advised.

"Wouldn't it be crazy to be talking to someone you can't see?" asked Chris.

"You don't have to talk to Him out loud; you can talk to Him in your heart. He knows how you feel, and He wants to help. I had similar questions as you have now when my dad died, but I remember how my father would talk to Him, and I decided to trust Him as my dad did. He brought peace in my heart, and I began to heal. Of course, as a family, we learned to lean on each other and talk our feelings through. That also helped me tremendously. Can I pray with you?"

"Please, do because I don't know what to say to Him."

After prayer, Chris' face seemed to lighten up a bit. A feeling of comfort went all over him. "Thank you, Jamie; I do not claim to have that peace you spoke about, but I do know that I feel better already. Let us focus on something more pleasant." The boys spoke about their dreams and aspirations and school. As it happened, they were at the same school, but they had never seen each other before.

"Well, I guess we can hang out some evenings, and I'll check up on you in school to see if you're okay."

"Thanks, Jamie; I do appreciate it," replied Chris.

"Boys, come on in; Karla is ready to go, and you have school in the morning," Jack called. It was almost eight in the evening, and the boys had not kept track of time. "Thanks again, Jamie; I sure do appreciate the time spent with you."

Karla, Mark, Jamie, and Maria thanked the family for inviting them over and expressed their appreciation for the dinner.

"Oh, we forgot to cut the cake," Susan exclaimed.

"That is okay," Karla replied. "I baked one for Mark and one for us, so enjoy it."

Lori was sad to see Maria go, but she knew she would see her at school the next day. Mark took them home, and Karla invited him to come in for the cake. She thanked him for the ride, and he expressed thanks for the cake. He was tempted to say something more to her but thought it would be premature. After bidding her goodbye, he got in his car and, with a wave of his hand, he drove off.

Karla called Maria and Jamie and thanked them for being so helpful to Lori and Chris. They talked a little bit about the day before Karla sent them to bed. "This was a good day," she sighed to herself. "I am glad we were able to help in a small way." Karla knew only too well how difficult the journey of healing would be. One day up, the other day down. But she was confident that healing would take place, and she was happy that Lori and Chris had found friends they could identify with who lived close by.

Chapter 20

Lori woke up early; she was surprised that she was looking forward to school. Although she had hung out with Angie, Brianna, and Terry, she never felt comfortable in the friendship. She was just trying to survive middle school the best way she knew how. She had pretended not to understand math to fit in with the group. *In retrospect, what a dumb thing to do,* she thought. *How could I have allowed myself to be pulled into such negativity? And to think I hurt so many people, including Maria. I am happy I met her, although I would have preferred if the circumstances were different.* Lori decided to try and pray; she did not know how but she remembered parts of the prayers prayed in church yesterday. "I will just start by thanking God for this morning and for my family and my new friend. I still do not understand why Joanna had to die, I miss her terribly, and sometimes I cannot stop crying, but I am going to try to trust You." She fumbled through the prayer and said, "God, I know

You understand, although it makes no sense to me; help me through this difficult time of my life."

In the Rodriquez household, Maria was also awake early. She was thinking about yesterday and wondered if she had helped Lori in any way. She got on her knees and prayed that Lori would have a good day and that Brianna and Angie would not bother any of them. *I know God loves them too, so I must pray for them to change. Change would come only when they are able to acknowledge what they did was wrong and desire to stop bullying others.* She wondered what their home life was like. *Were they bullied at home or in their community? Were they bullied in elementary school? What would cause someone to make another person's life a nightmare? I feel sorry for them,* she thought. Maria came back to reality when her alarm went off. "Time to get up," she said to herself. She would get dressed and help Jamie with the breakfast, spend some time with Mom, and be off to school on time.

As she made her way to the bus, she thought about the changes during the semester. She had started out with one friend, John, but now she had three more; Jackie, Lori, and Terry. She wondered what else she could do to help Angie and Brianna. She suspected that they would be more difficult to help because they might not see the need to change. "One cannot be helped if one does not want to be helped or, to put it another way, change cannot happen in a person's life if that person does not see the need to change," she said to herself. "But what if the person is afraid of change? This is not for me to decide," she said.

"Talking to yourself again, Maria," John laughed as Maria approached. She had not realized she was so close to the bus stop and that John was there.

"It is now part of who I am, I guess," she replied. "I didn't expect to see you taking the bus again this week."

"Oh, my mom is out of town at a training course for two weeks, so you have to put up with me another week."

"That's great for me but not so much for you."

"I don't mind, honestly, plus I get to spend some time with you. Here comes the bus."

She could see Terry coming in the distance, so she asked Mr. James to hold the bus for her. She sat beside John as usual and quietly shared with him her weekend activities. "That is great, Maria, I'm glad you have some new friends, and I am proud of you. You have been very busy helping others."

Terry boarded the bus and touched her on the shoulder as she passed. She turned and waved to her. "I believe this is going to be a good day," she remarked to John.

"I think so too," John replied. "Exams start next week, and I hope we are all ready for the state exams, especially Lori, who is trying to catch up on her assignments, study for exams, and still going through the grieving process."

"We are at school already! Come on; it's showtime."

As usual, Jackie's bus had pulled in ahead of them; Maria and Terry got off their bus and waited for Jackie. She always sat at the back of the bus and was one of the last students to get off. The girls made their way to classes chatting as they walked. They greeted Mr. Jones, went in, and sat down to the same routine of solving the two problems on the board while waiting for the bell to go. Lori came in, greeted them, and took her seat. She also settled down to solve the problems. Mr. Jones watched the girls and smiled to himself. *This is great,* he thought. In walked Brianna and Angie and started with their antics; they had no idea that Mr. Jones was watching them.

"Don't come in here with that," Mr. Jones stated. "You are not going to start any drama in my class. Sit down and work the problems."

The girls sheepishly went to their seats. The rest of the class filled in and began working the problems. The class went by quickly, and the rest of the day went by smoothly. Things were looking good, but Maria was not foolish enough to think that the girls would not try to get to her when she was alone. But, for now, things were good.

The girls met in the cafeteria for lunch, and they discussed the upcoming exams and how they could help each other prepare. They agreed to meet on Saturday at the library to prepare for the science and math exams.

They had to get permission from their parents or, in Jackie's case, her aunt. At the end of the day, they all made their way to either the car pick-up area or to the bus loop. It had been a great day.

The rest of the week went by quickly; all the girls had permission to meet at the public library at ten on Saturday morning. Lori's dad volunteered to pick up Maria and take her back home. Jackie's aunt would take her to and fro, but Terry would walk across since she lived close to the library. The session at the library was productive, and they were able to cover the areas in science where each person had weaknesses and solved some difficult math problems. The girls were proud of their accomplishments; they were ready for exams. They had fifteen minutes before pick-up time, and they spent the rest of the time talking, sharing their life ambitions, and planning for summer vacation meetings. They wanted to keep the friendship going throughout the summer and decided they would meet again to plan activities that their parents would approve and all of them could be involved.

Chapter 21

It was Sunday morning, and Karla reminded the children they were going to be picked up at 10:15 a.m. "Make sure you are ready; we must not keep them waiting," she remarked. Mark was a bit jealous that he was not the one picking them up, but he was happy that they did not have to take the bus.

The families had arranged to spend the afternoon together in the park, and they were all looking forward to being outdoors. Mark was also invited; it seemed he was becoming a part of their family. This was exciting to Maria as she jumped up with glee and thought to herself, *Maybe Mom is a little bit interested in Officer Mark. This is a good opportunity for them to get to know each other better. She would not be alone with him, and there was safety in numbers. It would be like a double date,* she thought. Maria burst out laughing, "A double date in a park." She was just happy that her mom had found some new friends, and she was smiling more often.

The families decided that Lori and Maria would be off taking photographs, Chris and Jamie would be riding, and the adults would be enjoying each other's company. There were lots of picnic tables and park benches along the trail and many opportunities for the adults to enjoy nature and its wonders. Life was getting to be good for Karla and her family.

The doorbell rang, and Maria rushed downstairs; her mom and brother were already at the door. She was happy to see Lori again. As girls would frequently do, they chatted all the way to church. Chris, on the other hand, was very quiet, as it appeared he did not want to go to church. Jamie tried to engage him in conversations, but he did not respond. Chris had a hard time dealing with Joanna's death. He looked at his family with disgust. *How could everyone be so happy when my little sister is in the cemetery six feet under? I do not understand. I cannot shake off the pain, and they are acting as if she did not even exist.* Jamie understood that Chris was going through a lot of inner turmoil. Boys tend to keep things in while girls will talk about their struggles. *How can I help Chris to understand that he needs to talk about his feelings, and it is okay to cry?* He prayed silently that God would use the pastor to bring a message of comfort, healing, and hope to Chris.

Jamie watched Chris as he got out of the car and made his way into the church. He made sure to sit beside him and told him he understood and that he would be there for him. The service started; the choir sang, but Chris' mind was far away. He could hear the choir singing, but he was not listening; he had no clue what the words of the song were. *Why am I here in church?* he thought. *Where was God when my sister needed Him? How can I serve a God who would allow my innocent little sister to die? He took out her light, and I am to serve Him.* Chris got up and walked out of the church. Jack and Jamie followed him out. Jamie put his arms around him and told him it was okay to cry, and it was part of the healing process. Jack stood by, not knowing what to say or do. He watched his son, and tears flowed down his cheek; he himself had not recovered from the loss, and he had cried many times in secret. He did not want his children to see him break down; he had to be strong for them. But he, too, needed healing. Jamie stepped back as Jack hugged his son. They cried together until there were no more tears. They stood there in each other's embrace until their bodies stopped shaking with grief. They dried their tears and smiled. "Let us go back in, son," Dad said.

Jamie had left them so they could grieve in private. They came back in and took their seats just as the pastor went up to preach. He spoke about God's infinite wisdom, "Trusting God even when we don't understand." Pastor Benjamin asked Mark to sing the song "Trust His Heart" by Babbie Y. Mason/Eddie Carswell. The chorus of the song was playing over and over in Chris' head. He did not understand it, but he sure was going to find out.

God is too wise to be mistaken.
God is too good to be unkind.
So, when you don't understand,
When you don't see His plan,
When you can't trace His hand, trust His heart.[1]

As Mark sang, tears began rolling down Lori's cheeks. The song had touched a nerve. Lori whispered to Maria, "How do we trust someone we don't know?"

"That is the key," remarked Maria. "You need to get to know Him first. When you do, He will teach you how."

Pastor Ben, as he was affectionately called, read from John 3:16, "For God so loved the world that he gave his only begotten Son, that whosoever believeth in him should not perish, but have everlasting life" (John 3:16, KJV). He spoke about God's love and faithfulness and why God chose to give His Son for us. "He gave His only Son to die for our sins. He did not have to, but He loved us so much that He was willing to suffer for us. God understands the loss of a child, a spouse, a parent, or friend; we don't understand why these things happen, but God knows why he allows things to happen in our lives."

Lori listened intently to the message she could not understand, and Maria suggested the family share their

---

1 Eddie Carswell/Babbie Mason, "Trust His Heart," track 1 on Trust His Heart, Spring Hill Music, 2009, digital download.

tragedy and their questions with the pastor and ask if they could meet him for some counseling sessions. "I'll discuss this with my parents," Lori responded.

Maria wondered if Lori's parents and brother were as confused as she was. If so, Pastor Ben would be the one to help. She would explain as much as she could, but ultimately her pastor was more equipped to deal with the counseling aspect of it.

Chris had been silent throughout the rest of the service; it appeared he was listening intently to everything Pastor Ben was saying. I am sure he too has questions, Maria thought. But unless he was willing to share his feelings with someone, no one could help him. She prayed silently, "God, intervene. Just like You helped us heal, bring healing to this family, and bring them through this very challenging time in their lives. Give them joy and let them laugh again."

The service ended, and Mark came over and greeted them; they sat and chatted for a while about the message. As they got up to leave, Pastor Ben came down the aisle and stopped to greet them. He greeted Mark, Karla, and her family, then turned his attention to Jack.

"Are you new to the church?"

"Yes, we are," Jack responded.

"I thought I saw you last week, but you left before I got a chance to introduce myself and welcome you. I am Pastor Ben; welcome to Changed Lives International Church."

“Thank you, I am Jack, and this is my wife Susan, our son Chris, and our daughter Lori.”

“A pleasure meeting you. I hope you enjoyed the service; we’d love to have you back. If you do not have a church home, you are welcome to worship here.”

“May I ask you a question?” Jack asked.

“Sure, go ahead,” Pastor Ben replied.

“I listened to your message today, and there are some things I don’t understand. You see, we just lost our little girl Joanna tragically, and we have a difficult time coping with the loss. As a matter of fact, I am still quite angry at God and wondered why He allowed this to happen. Is there any way you could help us understand better what you spoke about and guide us through this healing process?”

“Sure, I can; we can schedule a counseling session for you and your family. I am available on Mondays and Thursdays from five to eight in the evenings. Let me know which evening is convenient for you, and we can schedule an appointment. I am sorry for your loss; it is never easy to lose a loved one.”

Jack thanked Pastor Ben, shook his hands, and led the group out to the car.

“We have to get home and have dinner before we go to the park. We’ll see you at the park, Mark,” Jack stated. The drive home was quiet, everyone lost in their own thoughts, until Lori burst out, “Let us endeavor to enjoy ourselves this evening. It will be great going out with family and friends, plus I will get to take some photographs."

"Agreed," Chris replied. "Let's enjoy the day."

"We'll pick you up at three thirty," Jack announced as he pulled in the Rodriquez driveway.

"Thank you; we'll be ready when you get here."

They went in and quickly heated up the dinner they had cooked before going to church. Everyone was hungry; they hurriedly changed and rushed downstairs.

"This was difficult for Lori and her family, but I know it will get better," Maria remarked.

"Yes, I believe it will."

The family chatted a bit about the message, then ate in silence, each engaged in their own thoughts. After dinner, the three of them worked to clear and wash the dishes, with Karla suggesting they get some rest before they went to the park.

Jack picked them up at exactly three thirty. "A man of time," Karla remarked. Maria was excited to be going out with Lori. She anticipated that they would have a wonderful time. She would see Lori in action as she flashed that camera. Maria admired Lori's ability to capture the tiniest detail and thought it was interesting to see how she could catch a bird in flight.

Mark was already at the park when they got there. "Before you kids go off, let's decide the time and place to meet." It was decided they would meet at the table by the lake at seven o'clock. "Kids, this gives you exactly three hours to roam the park and do whatever you choose; just make sure you stay together at all times."

The boys rode off on their bicycles, and Lori and Maria went to explore the jogging trail and the rest of the park. Lori wanted to capture birds in flight, birds nesting, and anything else that would catch her imagination. The adults would walk, sit around, and talk. They would do whatever came to mind. Maria glanced back at her mom with a smile on her face. She hoped that her mother would get to know Mark more and that she would allow herself to love again.

The park was alive with activity, both wildlife and humans. "How wonderful it would be if we lived together in peace and harmony. That was God's intention, you know."

"What do you mean?" Lori responded.

Maria proceeded to tell her about the story of creation and the fall of man. "Read the book of Genesis; it is the first book in the Bible. It will tell you all you need to know about God's intention for us. But we had to spoil it. That is enough of my chatter; let us get to what we came here to do."

The girls walked quietly; they did not want to startle the birds with any sudden movement or loud noises. Lori explained the importance of being quiet so they did not disturb the nesting birds, "Because when we are quiet, the birds are calm, and we are able to see more of their habits."

"We may even catch a mother bird feeding her young."

"That would be cool; I've never seen that before," whispered Maria.

A squirrel darted across their path, and Lori was able to catch it in flight. She showed the photo to Lori, who was amazed at the speed at which Lori responded to an opportunity.

"This has been my hobby for as long as I can remember," Lori said. "I love nature, the birds, insects, animals, and our family likes nature walks, but I never thought of capturing their activity on camera," Maria responded.

Chris and Jamie sped off on their bikes, heading for the bike trail. Chris was riding fast and furious; he was trying to get the anger out of his system. He had bottled it up for the benefit of the family, and now he grasped the opportunity to let it out in his riding. Jamie had a hard time keeping up with him. He knew Chris needed time to process things and did not need to hear from him right now. When he was ready to talk, then he would listen, and he would only talk if Chris asked his opinion. They rode silently for forty-five minutes before Chris slowed down and came to a stop.

"Now I can talk," he said.

The boys got off their bikes and sat on the park bench under the trees where Chris talked, and talked, and talked. Jamie listened and only responded to questions Chris would pose. They talked about Joanna, the pain, God, and what it meant to be a Christian. Jamie answered questions as best as he could but referred Chris to study the Bible for himself. He told him that the church had a Bible study on Wednesday nights at seven; he had never attended, but maybe they both should go. Chris told him he would think about it and get back to him. It was time to go, and they headed to the place their parents had instructed them to meet.

They got there at five minutes past seven; they could see everyone was already there and ready to go. The boys apologized for their lateness, put their bikes on the van's bike rack, and climbed in. There were indications they all had a good time. Only Jamie knew the depth of pain Chris was going through. Mark waved goodbye, telling them he had a wonderful time, and thanked the families for including him in their plans.

"You are like family now," Karla said. Maria and Jamie exchanged glances, smiled, and winked at each other. Mark thanked Karla for being so gracious, waved again, went to his car, and drove off. "Time to go home; you have school tomorrow, and it's exam time. You need a good night's rest in preparation for your exams," Susan stated.

"Thank you, Jack and Susan, for the ride; we had a lovely time. We do appreciate your kindness." As the Rodriquez family got out of the car, Lori shouted, "See you tomorrow, Maria. We'll ace that test."

"Yes, we will," Maria replied.

Chapter 22

The girls, Maria, Lori, Terry, and Jackie, made their way to classes. The attendance would be taken, and then an announcement would come over the intercom for them to go to their testing locations. Only sixth-grade students were being tested today, and they would all be testing with their respective language arts teacher in that teacher's classroom. Jackie and Maria were testing together since they had the same language arts teacher while the other two girls would be testing with their respective teachers. Mr. Jones took the attendance and encouraged them to do their best on the exams. The announcements came on for the students who were testing to report to their testing locations; Mr. Jones gave them their tickets and wished them good luck.

The exam would last three weeks. There were days when they would not be testing, so they used those days to prepare for the next exam. The girls met at the library to prepare for the upcoming math and civics exams. They worked diligently, and all felt that they had done well on the exams. Terry and Lori were elated; they were confident of their success and looked forward to surprising their parents. They were back on track and intended to keep it that way.

The friendship between Maria, Jackie, Lori, and Terry grew. For the first time in middle school, Maria was enjoying every moment of it. "Who would have believed that I would enjoy being in school again?" Maria whispered under her breath. "Life certainly can throw in a few surprises." The girls decided they would FaceTime each other and plan to meet up sometime in the summer. Exams were finished, and they only had two more weeks left before the summer break. Jackie informed them that she would only be spending the first three weeks of the summer in Florida because she was going to spend the rest of the summer with her dad in New York.

"That means we must plan activities in those three weeks so Jackie could be a part of them," Maria concluded. The girls all agreed.

"What are some of the things we could do together that our parents would be in agreement with?" Lori asked. "Before we make any plans, I think we need to meet each other's parents, and our parents need to meet, so they are comfortable with us going out together. My parents are not going to allow me to go out with someone they do not know, even if Maria is there. They would want to meet my friends and their parents."

"I agree," chirped in Jackie. The other girls echoed their agreement. "Let us discuss our plan with our parents, and Jackie, you discuss it with your aunt, then we can finalize our plan for our families to meet at a place comfortable to all," Maria said. "Any suggestions? Terry, what do you think?" asked Maria.

"I think we could spend a day at the beach; that would be fun," Lori suggested.

They all agreed that it would be a fun thing to do. They discussed the various beaches and decided they preferred the beach in Delray. There are restaurants along the beach and one on the boardwalk; they have beach chairs, umbrellas, and picnic tables. There is even a volleyball court.

"Lots of fun activities for everyone. We could call it 'Friends and Family day,'" said Maria. They laughed at Maria's labeling of the day. Now they had to sell the idea to their parents.

"I think they will agree to the plan. None of us had any real friends before now, and our parents would be happy to know that we have found friends with similar values as our own," Jackie remarked.

The girls discussed the idea with their parents. Jackie's aunt wanted to discuss the plan with her father before coming to a decision; Terry's parents were a little hesitant at first, then agreed. Lori and Maria's parents agreed. It took one week for Jackie's aunt, Lisa, to agree;

at last, everyone was on board. The date was set for the Saturday before school closed. The girls were excited, and they could not wait for Saturday to arrive. None of them had ever been allowed to go out with friends before, so this was new to them. They had listened to other students boasting of where they went and who they met up with; these kids had listened but had nothing to add to any summer break discussions. They, for the most part, stayed home or went out with their immediate family.

Saturday finally came, and the families met each other at the beach. Lori's brother Chris, Maria's brother Jamie, Jackie's cousins Mark and Matthew, her aunt Lisa and her husband Pat, and Terry's brothers Dale and Tony came. The parents and children all chatted for a while until the boys indicated that they wanted to go play beach volleyball. The girls decided to swim, and the adults sat at one of the picnic tables under a tree. They needed to get to know each other before they decided on agreeing to the summer plans the girls had put forward to them. The girls kept looking back at the adults; they were curious to see whether the adults were getting along or not. They wanted them to like each other, so they would allow them to hang out as friends.

"Let us go sit with our parents for a while; then we can test the temperature of the conversations. This will give us a good idea of what their decisions would be," Terry said.

"I think we should just leave them to get to know each other and have a good time, just in case they don't agree, we would have spent one day together. Let us not worry about it and enjoy the moment," Maria replied.

The boys seemed to be having a good time, and the girls decided to join in the game with them. The parents were getting along well; they got to know each other a little. They spoke about making more time for their children and engaging in more family outings.

"It took our children to show us that we needed to spend more time with them and have fun as a family. I am happy for any opportunity where I can spend time with my children. In the past for me, it was always work, work, and more work," Jack said.

"We could plan a few outings like this where we all hang out together," Lisa responded. The parents agreed; also, they would be spending more time with their children, and they would allow their children to spend time with each other.

The group decided they would eat in one of the restaurants and make it a full day of fun, food, and fellowship. The day went by quickly and, soon, it was time to pack up and go. The parents informed the girls that they could go ahead and make plans to spend time together in the summer. They hugged each other and danced on the sand, then ran over to their parents and hugged them. Tired and happy, they bade each other goodbye and headed home.

Chapter 23

Summer was almost here, and Maria reflected on her first year in middle school. *What have I learned, and how have I impacted the people around me?* she asked herself. She reflected on the heartbreak and challenges she had faced during the school year and concluded that those difficult times were what helped her to see life from a different perspective. She had learned some valuable lessons; to forgive, to empathize, and to be tolerant of others. She understood that situations in life sometimes caused people to act or react in negative ways. She was one of those people who had reacted. She was grateful to Jamie, her mom, and John, who had encouraged her and let her know she was special and, most importantly, she was a child of the King, and she should behave as such. Her negative reactions could have resulted in destructive behaviors. Maria was grateful for her new friends, some of which had walked the same road as she did and behaved in a similar manner. Jackie was a good friend and support. They had all been changed; they had become better people.

The loss of her father and the grief that ensued had made her more sympathetic to others. She did not know what other students were going through, and she learned not to judge people before knowing their situation. Angie and Brianna were on her mind; she had tried to be friendly or at least civil to them, but they had responded negatively to her gestures. She wondered how she could help them; Maria decided to make one more attempt to engage them in a conversation with the hope that they would accept her invitation to put aside their differences. She had forgiven them for the way they had treated her and the rude comments they had passed about her. In retrospect, forgiveness was not difficult at all: you just had to make the decision to forgive and do it.

At school on Monday, Maria approached Brianna and Angie by greeting them, and they walked away from her without responding. Later in the hallway, she saw them again, but they verbally attacked her; they felt that Maria had stolen their friends. They threatened Maria and told her she would pay for what she had done and that next year would be another year. Maria responded by telling them she forgave them for all they had done to her and hoped they would forgive her for responding in negative ways. "I don't know what you are going through, but it is never okay to bully someone," she responded. For once, Angie was at a loss for words. She looked at Maria with sadness in her eyes and walked away.

"A soft answer turneth away wrath, but grievous words stir up anger." Maria now understood what it meant. "Daddy, thank you," she whispered. "It took me a long time to get it, but I now understand."

Maria did not know what the future held for her and her family; she only knew that she had formed the most unlikely friendships with girls who were once her tormentors. Her mother seemed to be healing, and it seemed that she was allowing Mark to be a part of her life. Jamie had found a friend in Chris, her mother had formed new friendships with her friends' parents, and life was good. What would the next school year bring? What would the future hold? Only time will tell.

Afterword

Tragedy has a way of leveling the playing field and opening opportunities for forgiveness and healing. Maria struggles with her father's favorite quote, "A soft answer turneth away wrath, but grievous words stir up anger." Unsure of its meaning, Maria seeks answers. Journey with her through tragedies, adversities, and anger as she unlocks the full meaning of the quote.

About the Author

Olive Peynado was born in Jamaica, West Indies. She worked as an educator in Jamaica and the USA for a total of thirty-one years. Olive has a master's degree in education and a bachelor's degree in accounting. She has worked with special needs and at-risk students in Florida Public School. Additionally, she has incorporated her Christian values in her profession to help students overcome life challenges and to blossom academically. Olive has a special place in her heart for children who have experienced life setbacks and has used her faith in God in an active role in helping them succeed. She enjoys teaching Sunday school and baking homemade Jamaican cakes for her family, friends, and members of her church. Currently, Olive is a retired middle school teacher in the state of Florida.

www.ingramcontent.com/pod-product-compliance
Ingram Content Group UK Ltd.
Pitfield, Milton Keynes, MK11 3LW, UK
UKHW020132250726
13967UKWH00002B/605

9 781685 562304